"This book is a gem. Undoubtedly, it will have a highly positive impact on the careers of many of its readers. It is packed with extremely sage advice on how to bring all major aspects of one's workaday life under firm control in the interest of the greatest possible job satisfaction and rapid advancement. It should prove invaluable for almost everyone on the job—entry level to midcareer."

> —RICHARD LATHROP
> Author of *Who's Hiring Who*

"If this book does nothing more than to stimulate people to look at their jobs and their relationships with their colleagues in a more penetrating and sensitive way, it will be well worth reading and pondering. Wachtel livens his book with many relevant anecdotes drawn from his broad experience as a personnel executive and as a consultant. There will be few readers who will not recognize the situations he describes and benefit from the insights he displays."

> —EDWARD ROBIE
> President, Group Moves and Consulting Services
> Merrill Lynch Relocation Management

"*How to Hold On to Your Job* is worth its weight in paychecks! Anyone can quickly benefit from its down-to-earth advice. An absolute must if you are seriously interested in career development."

> —DON GERMAN
> Coauthor of *How to Find a Job When Jobs are Hard to Find*

"In the '60s and '70s, the road to success was travelled by job-hopping from company to company. Times have indeed changed, and the senior management of the 1990s will be drawn from that cadre of people who are smart enough to succeed in their own organizations today. Some of Eric Wachtel's guidance may make you bristle, but *hear him*. He's telling you to pay attention in new ways, to look at your workplace with a more objective eye, focused on the long term benefits of smart thinking now."

> —DR. DOREEN V. BLANC
> Chase Manhattan Bank

HOW TO HOLD ON TO YOUR JOB

S. Eric Wachtel

M. Evans and Company, Inc.
New York

Library of Congress Cataloging in Publication Data

Wachtel, S. Eric.
How to hold on to your job.

Includes index.
1. Vocational guidance. 2. Job security. I. Title.
HF5381.W153 1983 650.1′4 83-16408

ISBN 0-87131-419-3 (pbk.)

M. Evans and Company, Inc.
216 East 49 Street
New York, New York 10017

Design by Lauren Dong

Manufactured in the United States of America

9 8 7 6 5 4 3 2 1

To the memory of Paul Bohne, Sr.,
friend, mentor, dowser, and
Man for All Seasons

Thanks to Max Gunther, whose assistance in writing this
book was invaluable.

Contents

1

Surviving in a Tough Environment

We are living in hard times. No adult needs to be told this. It certainly is not news to the millions of Americans, Canadians, and Europeans who are unemployed. Nor is it news to most of those who still cling to their jobs. For there is fear in the air. Everyone feels it, from the lowest-paid clerk in the mailroom all the way up to the company president. In today's cruel economic world, *anyone's* job can be snatched away at any time.

News reports in the past few years have tended to emphasize the plight of unionized blue-collar workers, for their woes often make shocking headlines. It is compellingly dramatic when General Motors shuts down a production line and lays off three thousand men and women in one terrible blow. It is not as dramatic when a struggling company tightens its belt and phases out a few jobs in the advertising and accounting departments. That kind of small, quiet episode doesn't make good TV material—but to the people phased out, and to those left wondering who will be next, it is an experience full of the most stark terror.

Multiply that obscure little episode by the thousands, the hundreds of thousands, and you have a major world and national problem.

White-collar people, most of them lacking unions or any other special protection, make up about half the total of unemployed—and they are my special concern. As a management consultant involved in executive-recruitment for clients, I'm in a good position to feel winds of change in the white-collar job market. I've never seen it as bad as it is today. My company isn't an employment agency and doesn't solicit job applications or career résumés, but I now find myself half buried in them.

There is a certain tone of desperation in many of the letters that pour onto my desk each week. "Please help me," begs a forty-year-old man who has just lost a middle-management job and cannot find another. "I don't know where to turn," says a young woman who fears her once-promising job with an architectural firm is about to be abolished.

These are, without doubt, the hardest times since the Great Depression of the 1930s. A job is no longer an inalienable right, something every high-school graduate takes for granted. There is no more guaranteed job security. Not today. A job, today, is something you keep as long as you are lucky.

Or smart.

I am going to show you how to be smart.

In a hotel dining room one night not long ago, I inadvertently overheard part of a conversation at the next table. There were three people at that table: a man of perhaps sixty and a younger man and woman, both in their thirties. The older man was lecturing; the younger people were listening deferentially. Because of facial resemblances, I surmised that they were a family group, a father and his son and daughter.

The older man was delivering a standard fatherly lecture on the facts of business life. "All you need to keep in mind is one thing," he said earnestly. "Just learn your job. That's all. Learn to do it better than anybody else. Nothing else counts. Never mind getting involved in office politics and all that. Just master your job so well that nobody can ever take it away from you. That's it in a nutshell—the surest prescription for success."

The younger man and woman were obviously not completely convinced. They needled the older man with questions and gently cynical comments, and they offered details of their own job experiences that seemed to contradict what he had said. In the end, he backed down a little and admitted that he might have stated the case somewhat too baldly. "It isn't all that black-and-white," he agreed. "There are gray areas." But he stood by his basic statement. The younger man and woman finally subsided into puzzled silence.

I understood their dilemma perfectly. Should they believe their father, obviously a man of long, rich, and varied experience in the business world? Or should they believe their own firsthand observations?

The father's statement could not be dismissed lightly, for it was not based only on his own experience. It had the weight of tradition behind it; it sounded something like a Great Truth. It was a preachment right out of the old Work Ethic. Keep your nose to the grindstone. Do your own job and do it well; never mind what anybody else is doing. Whatever your job is, become superior at it. If you're good, the world will recognize it and reward you.

As the father defended this preachment, the tone of doubt seeping into his voice made me think he didn't wholly believe it either. He, too, seemed puzzled. The problem was that he had learned his basic career lessons in an environment that was profoundly different from the one we struggle in today. The 1950s, 1960s, and early 1970s were years of virtually nonstop boom—the longest and most extravagant boom ever enjoyed by this country or any country. In a time like that, Horatio Alger teachings make good sense. Virtue does get rewarded. The dedicated employee who attends to the grindstone does, in time, earn raises and promotions. The pie is so big that there is a piece for everybody. Companies, buoyed by ever-expanding markets, can afford to be generous. People jockey for job positions and career advantages, but this jockeying lacks the desperate quality that can be seen at other times. If you lose out in one scramble, you plunge into another. Or if you choose to ignore the jockeying altogether—as the father urged his son and daughter—it can hardly hurt you and may even help.

Today, none of the above applies.

Let me tell you two stories of life as it is *really* lived in the 1980s. The first story concerns a woman. Call her Jeanne. (As will be true of all case stories in this book, I draw her from my actual experience but feel obliged to disguise her identity.) Jeanne had a lower-level management job in a large company's marketing department. She was technically more than competent; she was so good at her job that some even called her a genius. However, she was clumsy socially. She tended to irritate people with her mannerisms, and sometimes she hurt them—not through any basic lack of kindness, but simply by not paying attention. She felt so secure in her job competence—which was indeed impressive—that she felt no need to study the ebb and flow of personal events around her.

"So-and-so's opinion doesn't concern me in the slightest," she would often say loftily—so often that people mimicked her saying it when she was not around. She would point to a sheaf of papers and ask belligerently, "Were my figures correct or weren't they?" Of course, they always were. She believed that was enough.

She had an assistant and understudy named Ruth. Ruth lacked Jeanne's technical competence. Indeed, the fact should be stated a little more bluntly: Ruth's job performance was only mediocre. She made frequent mistakes. When this happened, however, she found other people willing to help her patch things up. For Ruth paid close attention to the people around her and the complex structure of job and personal relationships in which they all worked.

One day, while making a presentation to a management group, Jeanne criticized a divisional vice-president for his poor understanding of certain market undercurrents that were threatening to hurt the company. She was perfectly correct: the man did not have a good grasp of market undercurrents. By failing to act against them when they first became apparent, he had allowed a trivial problem to become a grave one. But there are good and bad ways to approach a situation in which you believe a superior is messing up his job, and Jeanne had chosen the very worst one. She stood up and expressed her views bluntly and publicly.

Over the next few weeks, if she had been alert to such things, she would have noticed certain warning signals. People began going to lunch without her. Conversations seemed to stop abruptly when she entered a room. Her name appeared to be slowly fading from various circulation lists, with the result that fewer and fewer memos and other materials came to her desk.

She went on insisting that other people's opinions did not concern her. She was still saying this on the day she was told she no longer had a job.

Her boss put it as gently as he knew how. He mumbled about "restructuring" and "phasing out." But it was all a kindhearted lie. Jeanne was being fired, plainly and simply. Ruth took over her title immediately.

The second story deals with a man I'll call Dan. He, like Jeanne, came to a stage in his career when he began to receive warning signals that his job was in jeopardy. Unlike Jeanne, he took the signals seriously and did something about them.

Dan was an executive with responsibilities in the area of finance. The company for which he worked had run into hard times during the middle 1970s. By the early 1980s the company was in real trouble. Its markets were shrinking. Its cash-flow problems were appalling. The directors had cut the common stock dividend three times in an attempt to conserve cash, but nothing seemed to do any good. The stock price had been sliding downward inexorably for years. Major stockholders were screaming. Everybody was mad at everybody else. Blame was being thrown in all directions like mud. A large glob of it landed on Dan—not because he deserved it, but because he happened to be a handy target. The company president and other senior executives, struggling desperately to save their own skins, blamed Dan for some faulty decisions in which he had played only a minor role. Some of the decisions, in fact, had been basically made before he even joined the company.

Recognizing that it would be useless to protest, Dan kept his mouth shut and waited to see if the air would clear, as sometimes happens in such situations. It did not happen. Instead, Dan began to notice more and more alarming signals. Senior executives failed to return his phone calls. A more or less monthly invitation to lunch with the president failed to materialize. There was a definite coolness in the office atmosphere.

But the loudest signal of all was Dan's accidental discovery that the president had called in an executive-search firm. The firm's assignment: find somebody to replace Dan.

Dan's first angry instinct was to quit on the spot. It would have been satisfying to tell everyone what he thought of them and then walk out. But Dan had learned early in life that temper tantrums, while they let off steam and feel good momentarily, seldom accomplish much in the way of solid, long-term resolution of problems. And so he cooled himself. He took a long weekend. He spent three days talking with his wife, playing with his kids, ambling about by himself, thinking. Piece by piece, he developed a plan.

It was a two-part plan. One part was designed to save the company. The other part was designed to save himself.

Over the next few weeks, Dan got together with bankers and divisional finance people. He presented them with some new ideas he had worked out for raising cash. Dan's show of initiative and his seeming optimism—which, in truth, he did not feel—lifted many of those people out of a swamp of dull despair in which they had been mired for years. They took his basic ideas, added to them, sharpened them, and improved them.

Dan then arranged a morning meeting with the president and told him about the new ideas. The president listened, astonished. If you had asked him, he would have guessed that morale in the company was so low that nobody had the energy to generate useful new ideas. Everybody was too busy trying to dodge the blame that was being hurled around—and that included the president.

Dan had thought long and hard about this meeting, and he conducted it with the greatest care. He said nothing about being unhappy. He uttered no protests over unfair treatment. He did not mention the secret executive search that he had discovered. Instead, calmly and quietly, he explained his ideas and gave the thoughts of the bankers and divisional finance people he had been talking to.

The president asked questions. Dan had anticipated them and was able to answer them tellingly. Finally the president nodded and said, "Yes, I've got to say these ideas are worth trying. So go ahead, try them and see what happens."

As Dan was walking out the door, the president called him back and asked, "You free for lunch?"

The story ended happily. Dan's ideas worked. Today he is the company's senior vice-president in charge of finance. It would be an exaggeration to say the company is once again enjoying unrestrained growth. The company has had to struggle hard to reach a state of good financial health, and the struggle continues—but the stock price is once again on the rise.

Dan's struggle continues also. I talk to him once in a while, and I know he will never relax his vigilance. He knows as well as anybody that it is not enough today simply to master your job. You must also be ready to do whatever is necessary to hold on to it.

That is what this book is about: holding on to your job in a hard, hard environment.

Combing the business literature, past and present, I find that very little has been written on this subject. There is voluminous material on the techniques of landing a *new* job, but the topic that fascinates me—preserving and improving what you've got—has been but sparsely covered.

I'm not sure why. I suspect the reason may be that, to many who have taken only a casual look at it, the subject seems intimidatingly complex.

In some ways it *is* complex. If it were simple, people would figure it all out for themselves, and I would feel no need to write a book about it. The fact is that only a minority of employed people seem to have an instinctive grasp of the precepts I am about to discuss. These precepts are not hard to understand, but they are not obvious to most people—which is why I feel I can perform a useful service by explaining the precepts in a clear, organized form.

How did I learn them? By studying individual careers—hundreds of careers—close up.

I have been in personnel work of one kind or another throughout my business life. I've worked for large organizations such as Gulf + Western and the American Stock Exchange. I am now head of my own management consulting company, which, among its activities, conducts executive searches and evaluations of corporate departments. All along the way, I've hunted for the differences between winners and losers in business.

When I was a young man, just starting out, I harbored the Horatio Alger notion that it is enough simply to know one's own job and mind one's own business. This notion was knocked out of my head by a man who breezed confidently into the company where I worked, established himself quickly as a climber, and shot up like a rocket. He was a man whose job competence was merely average. Yet he overtook many men and women of what I considered greater job talents. Before long, people far older than he and with many more years of job seniority were reporting to him.

I puzzled over his story for a long time. I talked to him and to people who knew him. I probed and pondered. I observed that, in some seemingly magical way, he moved rapidly to the front rank as he attained each new job level. He might be the junior person in a certain department in terms of time on the job, yet he was never among those weeded out in times of trouble and retrenchment. Somehow he made himself too valuable to dismiss or demote.

Too valuable to whom? In what ways? What magical umbrella of protection did he raise over his head?

Gradually, puzzling over these questions, I began to understand what it was he did that other people did not do. I began to apply my growing understanding to my own career, and over the years I studied other people's careers—the successes, the failures, and the near-misses—to see whether the same lessons applied to everyone.

They do. The precepts are universal.

The *technical* aspects of various jobs differ widely. A financial analyst, an advertising supervisor, and a production engineer might have a hard time explaining to each other what they do all day long, yet the forces of the job environment act on all of them in the same way. Similarly, a newcomer fresh from college might feel his or her job problems differ greatly from the problems faced by a mid-career veteran. Not so. The same basic precepts apply to both.

This book is for you no matter what kind of job you hold, what kind of company you work for, or what industry it is in. But the book is *particularly* for you if you are uneasy about the future.

Perhaps your industry is in less than robust health. Your company is fighting for survival. You lack the comfortable feeling that your job is perfectly secure. If so, join the club—and read on.

I must warn you that you will not find quick fixes or Band-Aid approaches in this book. The process of building job security takes time. Not a great deal of time—perhaps only a few months—but it cannot be accomplished instantly. If you fear you are going to be fired or laid off or demoted next week, I can only suggest that you turn immediately to Chapter 16, "If All Else Fails." That chapter proposes last-ditch emergency measures—the book's closest approach to a quick fix. Having pulled yourself through the emergency, you can then study the rest of the book and prepare for a happier experience in your next job.

This book will show you how to raise an umbrella of protection over yourself. It does not guarantee to give you *perfect* security. Perfect security is a myth; it exists only in dreams and life-insurance ads. What these precepts *will* do for you is make you far safer in your job than you have ever been before. By the time you finish the book, you will know how to make the job environment push you up, not out.

═Vulnerability Quiz═

Are you safe in your job? Or are you in danger of losing it—and, if so, how great is the danger? This evaluation will help you arrive at some insights. It will tell you how hard you need to work on the precepts of this book.

Both the test and this book are designed to help you read the danger signals and build security. Study the test carefully. You may be surprised. You are probably more vulnerable than you think.

1. When was your last title change?
   In the last 18 months   Score 5 __
   Between 18 months and 3 years ago   3 __
   More than 3 years ago   1 __
   I've never had my title changed.   0 __

2. When and how big was your last pay increase?
   It was in the last 12 months and was substantial.   Score 5 __
   It was in the last 2 years.   3 __
   It was more than 2 years ago.   1 __
   My pay hasn't changed since I started this job.   0 __

3. When did you last receive some indication of in-
   creased status—for example, a bigger office, rede-
   coration of your office, a reserved parking space?
   In the last 2 years   Score 5 __
   Between 2 and 4 years ago   3 __
   Longer than that   1 __
   I can't remember ever being upgraded in this way.   0 __

4. How would you describe your feelings of excitement
   or boredom with your job?
   It's endlessly exciting and stimulating.   Score 5 __
   It's exciting most of the time.   3 __
   It's usually boring. There are some exciting days.   1 __
   It's tedious. I can't wait for quitting time.   0 __

5. How would you describe your feelings on awakening
   on a typical weekday?
   Raring to go; can't wait to get to the office.   Score 5 __
   I look forward to getting to work on most days.   3 __
   I often feel weary and uninspired, want to stay in
   bed.   1 __
   I hate getting up on weekdays.   0 __

6. When your boss circulates memos, where does your
   name appear on the distribution list?
   Usually at or near the top   Score 5 ___
   Usually at or near the bottom   3 ___
   At the bottom when it appears at all   1 ___
   I never receive any but all-staff memos.   0 ___

7. How often do people at the office ask for your opinion?
   Often   Score 5 ___
   Sometimes   3 ___
   Rarely   1 ___
   Never   0 ___

8. How often does your boss commend you for your
   work?
   Often   Score 5 ___
   Sometimes   3 ___
   Once in a great while   1 ___
   I can't remember ever hearing a word of praise.   0 ___

9. How often do you and your boss get together to chat
   over lunch, a drink, a cup of coffee, a walk, or similar
   informal occasions during working hours?
   Often   Score 5 ___
   Sometimes   3 ___
   Rarely   1 ___
   My boss and I have never had a long, casual chat.   0 ___

10. When was the last time your boss invited you to a
    meeting or business/social gathering with other man-
    agement people?
    Within the past 3 months   Score 5 ___
    Within the past year   3 ___
    More than a year ago   1 ___
    I've never been invited to any such gathering.   0 ___

11. How would you describe your boss in terms of his
    or her standing in the company?
    Powerful, respected, in or headed for top manage-
    ment   Score 5 ___
    Seems to have some power; standing is unclear   3 ___
    Seems to have little power, low status   1 ___
    Powerless, ignored, dead-ended   0 ___

12. Do you have a mentor—that is, somebody with in-
    fluence in the company who takes a genuine interest

in your career and whom you can count on to help
and protect you?

Yes, I have a mentor.	Score 5 __
I think I have but I'm not sure.	3 __
There's a person who seems to like me, but we don't have much contact.	1 __
Management people don't know I exist.	0 __

13. In your job, how wide and varied are your contacts
with other parts of the company?

I'm in contact with all levels of the company.	Score 5 __
I occasionally deal with people at higher levels.	3 __
I deal only with people on my own level or below.	1 __
I almost never see anybody outside my own task group.	0 __

14. Have you been given leadership responsibilities?

Yes, I'm in a leadership position or am frequently assigned to projects in which I lead others.	Score 5 __
Once in a while I've headed small task groups.	3 __
I'm seldom asked to lead a group.	1 __
I've never had any leadership experience.	0 __

15. How often do you make recommendations that get
implemented?

I more or less expect that the majority of my recommendations will be implemented.	Score 5 __
I've had some of my recommendations implemented.	3 __
I seldom make recommendations because the odds are they won't be implemented.	1 __
I've never made a recommendation. If I did, it would be ignored.	0 __

16. How well do you feel you are known around the
company?

Many people on all levels know me well.	Score 5 __
I'm fairly well known.	3 __
I'm relatively unknown.	1 __
Nobody outside my department even knows my name.	0 __

17. How easily can you get in to see your boss or talk
to him or her on the phone?

My boss either talks to me immediately or, if tied up, gives me a call later in the day.	Score 5 __
Sometimes I have to wait a day or so.	3 __

I'm usually made to wait and sometimes must repeat
my request for some of my boss's time.   1 —
My boss has no time for me.   0 —

18. How would you describe the relationship between
yourself and your boss?
   Mutually respectful, friendly, relaxed   Score 5 —
   Courteous but reserved   3 —
   Strictly businesslike, structured, lacking warmth   1 —
   What relationship?   0 —

19. When was the last time your boss or anybody else
discussed career goals and promotional opportuni-
ties with you?
   During the past year   Score 5 —
   Two or 3 years ago   3 —
   Longer than that   1 —
   During my initial interview for this job   0 —

20. What is the condition of your company?
   Stable and growing   Score 5 —
   Stable but not growing   3 —
   Contracting, selling off or closing operations   1 —
   Unstable, troubled, fighting for life   0 —

SCORING

96–100	Unusually secure
90–95	Relatively secure
80–89	Moderately vulnerable
60–79	Vulnerable
40–59	Highly vulnerable
Below 40	In imminent danger

2

Taking Stock
of Yourself

The late Ward Howell, considered by many to be the founding father of the executive-recruitment profession, watched thousands of people scrambling up the ladders of their careers. The thing that surprised him most about this restless panorama, he said more than once, was the degree to which people in the business world left their fate to chance.

"Business people could learn a lot from athletes," he used to say. "An athlete trains himself very carefully, grooms himself for the competition he's got to face. He also *studies* himself. He's always weighing himself, testing his wind, his strength. He looks for weak places in himself and then tries to strengthen them. He looks ahead to competitors he'll come up against, tries to find what their strengths and weaknesses are. He drills himself for every possible situation: if *this* happens, he'll do *that*. An athlete really prepares. But people in the business world mostly just grope around, taking whatever comes to them. Why aren't they as careful as athletes? A business career is just as tough as an athletic career—and it lasts a lot longer."

Howell's question is a good one. Why don't people take stock of themselves as jobholders, strengthen their weak points, plan and prepare for future competitions? Perhaps the reason is that people are intimidated by the business world's complexity. So many factors influence job success or failure that it is hard to arrive at a reasonable plan of preparation and self-testing, the way an athlete does.

I agree that it is hard. But it is not by any means impossible. You can take stock of yourself right now by asking yourself the eight questions below. The questions will help you identify weaknesses— and once having identified them, of course, you should immediately get to work and start supplying what is missing.

The end result will be preparation: an increased ability to withstand shocks and to grasp opportunities. I don't mean that you will be shock-proof. Nobody is. The best-trained athlete has a bad day once in a while, loses his cool, makes mistakes. You are not immune to misfortune. No matter how well prepared you are, you are still going to be hit by bad luck once in a while, and you are also going to make mistakes. We all do.

But bear this in mind: rarely is anybody's job security threatened or career damaged by one mistake. What puts you in jeopardy is a long history of making mistakes. By regularly taking stock of yourself and keeping up your strengths, you can greatly improve your chances of keeping your paycheck and eventually winning bigger ones.

These are the eight key questions:

1. *Is your education adequate for your present job and the jobs you hope to rise into? More specifically, how does your education compare with that of other men and women around you, or those doing similar work in other companies?*

Remember that any of those people, even if they aren't direct competitors today, could come up against you in some future race for a coveted job in your field. Educational attainment counts heavily when management is trying to decide among job candidates. I've seen many promising careers stalled because of a weakness in this area. Indeed, I know of at least one company that used education as a key criterion in deciding whom to lay off during a 1982 cutback. Several hundred white-collar people were to get the axe. In trying to decide which ones, the company rated each employee on the basis of what was called "value to us," or VTU for short. Your numerical VTU score determined whether you stayed or went. Educational accomplishment was heavily weighted in making up the score.

So seek extra education even though it means some hardship. Sure, the hours of study seem long and onerous; the fees are hard to bear; the course looks difficult; you feel you can barely understand the textbook after a hard day at the office. No matter. Do it anyway.

You should never forget this one point: you may not be willing to put up with the hardship, but there will always be somebody else who is.

2. *Are you staying abreast of technological changes that bear on your work?*

I know a woman who worked for the same company for many years and believed she was invincible. On the face of things, she seemed to have a point. She had risen over the years to the job of head bookkeeper, and she boasted—accurately, for all I know—that she knew more about the company's financial affairs than the president did. "There's no way they could ever let me go," she would say when conversations turned to worried speculation about the company's future. "I'm needed too much."

Holding this dangerous belief, she scorned the idea of updating her technological training. When word processors and other mysterious pieces of equipment began to turn up in accounting departments in the 1970s, she didn't bother to familiarize herself with the hardware and its uses. She even stayed away when the company she worked for offered employees a free word-processor training course on company time.

A day came when all the knowledge that was in her head—knowledge that she alone had once commanded—was stored in magnetic tapes, disks, and other electronic memories. The information could be retrieved by anybody who knew how to use the equipment, including a junior bookkeeper who had troubled to take the offered training.

The head bookkeeper was no longer indispensable. Her salary was high, but the company did not really need to pay it.

It was only a matter of time before someone realized this and acted on it. During a period of sagging earnings, the company president ordered a weeding-out of higher-salaried people whose grand paychecks could not be justified. The head bookkeeper today holds a job behind the cash register of a cafeteria.

The moral: listen, read, and act. We live in an era of bewilderingly rapid technological change. It is your obligation to yourself to be constantly aware of changes that are affecting or will one day affect whatever work you do. Talk to others in your field; listen carefully when they tell of new technologies they have encountered or read about. Do your own reading, particularly in publications devoted to your field. All trade and professional journals pay attention to developing new technologies that bear on their readers' lives. Ask yourself whether you are prepared for the changes that may creep over your job next year or ten years hence—and if you are not prepared, do something about it before you get beached.

Many companies offer free or low-cost training to employees who want to learn new technologies. In addition, companies that sell new technologies—IBM, GTE, Xerox—continually offer seminars for employees of customer companies. Many professional societies also offer training courses to their members from time to time. For example, consider the National Shorthand Reporters Association, a society of people who record court trials and business meetings. This work once was done entirely by hand; then two great technological advances occurred. The first was the technique of tape recording, and then came video recording. In each case, the association set up workshops to help its members learn to handle the unfamiliar new equipment.

If you have even a faint suspicion that some such technological wave is going to wash over you, get yourself the needed training as fast as you can. (If that is impractical for some reason and if there is no other alternative, as a last resort you can get yourself transferred to a different kind of work. We will discuss this sometimes dangerous move in another chapter.)

Don't be hesitant about asking your boss's cooperation in your attempt to prepare for technological change. If you approach the situation in the right way, you score points for yourself by requesting the company's help.

Avoid two things. First, don't phrase the request so as to make it sound like a personal indulgence: "I wonder if I could have a few days off. There's this seminar..." Second, don't phrase it in terms of what you feel is owed to you: "Seems to me the company has a responsibility to help employees stay on top of things... After all, *you* get to go to a lot of seminars and study groups..."

Instead, the main point to concentrate on is that you want to make yourself more valuable to the company—and to your boss. Try to put this point across in an easy and natural way: "Big changes are coming. It seems to me we might be in trouble around here if nobody understands this new equipment. I've done some studying in my spare time, but I feel I need some hands-on training. GTE is offering a three-day seminar next week..."

Some companies are more open to such requests than others, of course. Perhaps you work for a small company that simply cannot afford to grant employees a lot of time off or pay many tuition bills. This may make your campaign harder, but it should not discourage you.

In a situation like this, the best approach is to research all available educational offerings *thoroughly* before going to your boss with a request for help. Don't just go up to him or her with a vague ambition: "I feel I need some more accounting courses... I was hoping the company would help me." Instead, find out exactly what is available at local schools, colleges, and other institutions. Find out what it will cost. Figure out how much of that cost you can carry yourself. Determine whether the course will overlap with working hours and if so to what degree. Shop around until you have put the best possible package together. And then, and only then, go to your boss with a statement of precisely and specifically what you want and why.

If the company still won't help you, take the course anyway.

3. *Are you sure the job you are doing is the job your boss and those above him want done?*

In a time of fast change such as the present, organizations adapt raggedly and unevenly. One part of the organization may stay abreast of the changes and perhaps even a step or two ahead, while other parts lag behind to various degrees. This can have a profound and upsetting effect on people's jobs.

Examine the job you've been doing. Perhaps you were given

your basic instructions by a previous boss. Your present boss may have different goals, different instructions from above, or simply a different way of looking at things. He or she hasn't yet given you any new instructions—perhaps doesn't realize they are needed, or hasn't figured out what the new procedures should be. Whatever the cause is, *you might be doing your job wrong.*

Or perhaps your entire group or department has failed to keep up with change. You may be doing precisely what your boss wants, but he or she may be wrong. The work being delivered by your team is not being received gratefully upstairs.

Whatever lies behind the problem, your job is in jeopardy if you no longer produce what needs to be produced.

I recall an episode that took place in a medium-sized insurance company. In the early 1980s this company was troubled, as were many of its competitors, by a growing problem in collecting premiums. Laid-off people couldn't afford to pay, and alarming numbers of policies were lapsing. Struggling to maintain headway in this tough environment, the company had begun to experiment with a lot of innovations designed to help both its straitened policyholders and itself.

Top management wanted weekly reports on how these innovations were working. One set of reports was supposed to come from a small team of people headed by a man I will call Joe Prince. His chief lieutenant was a young woman. One of the main duties of her job, as she saw it, was to prepare those reports.

As time went by, however, she saw that she could relax. Joe Prince was an affable fellow who preferred delivering reports in person rather than in written form. His practice was to gather the relevant figures informally and then, just as informally, give the gist to his superiors at lunch or over drinks. This seemed to satisfy everybody. The young woman stopped preparing reports and was glad to have the extra time.

Then Joe Prince was recruited away from the company. A new man named Henry Barker was moved into Joe's office. Henry Barker was a taciturn, somewhat cold man, not very well liked by the genial top-management group but admired for his superior grasp of complicated insurance-industry problems. He and the young woman developed a courteous but not friendly relationship.

Nobody in top management bothered to tell him about the reports his group was supposed to produce. Perhaps nobody really needed the information for a time; it wasn't missed. But then, suddenly, a senior vice-president realized he needed it for a forthcoming presentation. Where was it?

Henry Barker was called upstairs for a painful interview. He then went back downstairs and loaded all the blame on the young woman.

"You knew you were supposed to turn out those reports!" he shouted. "You were hoping you could duck the work and I'd never find out about it, right?"

"No, that isn't true. Joe Prince—"

"Never mind Joe Prince! It was your responsibility to stay on top of things like this . . ."

She was not fired right away. But Henry Barker made her life so miserable from then on that a blowup was inevitable. It came a few weeks later, and as far as I know she has been jobless ever since.

You must protect yourself against such changes in and around your job. The best protection is communication, and a close second is alertness. Talk often with your boss and with others who depend on or have some practical interest in what you do. Keep asking if you are actually doing what people want done.

You don't have to ask it so often as to make a nuisance of yourself; nor should you ask it in such a way that you seem to be soliciting words of praise. Just once in a while, when a natural moment comes, say to your boss: "There are several different ways to put this kind of report together. I've been doing it this one way all along, but it occurred to me that maybe you'd find another way more useful for your purposes. Do you have a few minutes . . . ?"

Never get so comfortable in a routine that you fail to notice changes happening or impending. Never stop asking, looking, and listening.

4. *Have you made yourself known as somebody who is willing to take on extra work and increased responsibilities?*

One of the least loved figures in the business world is the time-server—the man or woman who plods through each day with no real sign of interest, does exactly what is required, never any more, and is out the door within ten seconds of closing time each afternoon.

Don't ever let yourself become that kind of drone. In good economic times companies tolerate such people because they don't actually do any harm. They perform their assigned work more or less reliably if well supervised, and in many operations they are the bulk of the work force. But they are always among the first to be let go in troubled times, and as a rule they get no more than routine raises and promotions.

The person who attracts attention is the one who shows interest in the work, the one who doesn't mind taking on an extra burden once in a while. It has never been known to kill anybody to stay in the office once in a while for an unscheduled and unpaid half-hour. It *has* been known to help people's careers a great deal.

If your boss asks you to take on some irritating little task and indicates that there is no hurry, don't do what most would do: put it off, hope it gets forgotten, then reluctantly tackle it after a second or third reminder. Surprise your boss by doing it right away, even if you have to stay late to fit it into your schedule. Then march into your boss's office the next day, conduct some other business, and on your way out pause at the door and say, "Oh, by the way, I took care of that problem about the missing order forms . . ."

That is the kind of subordinate who gets somewhere.

I would even counsel you to take on trivial, personal chores if your boss or some other executive asks you to. Suppose the executive vice-president stops by your desk and says, "Listen, I wonder if I could ask a favor? My daughter arrives at the airport tomorrow evening around six, but I'll be tied up at a meeting till a couple of hours later. I wonder if you could meet her and take her to some nice place for dinner—on me, of course. I know it's an imposition, and if you can't make it, of course I'll understand . . ."

Like hell he'll understand.

Don't whine, don't grimace, don't squirm, don't make excuses about the studying you've got to do. Just smile pleasantly and say, "Sure, it'll be a pleasure."

Some would object to this as apple-polishing. (There are also, of course, some less elegant phrases to describe it.) Some would consider it beneath their dignity. Some would huff, "I'm hired to work in the paralegal department, not to be a baby-sitter!" This is true, perhaps. To do such favors for a superior may needle one's pride a little. But is your pride really so tender that you would favor it over your job security?

If the executive vice-president made a routine out of asking such favors—if he tried to turn me into his family's regular airport meeter—then I would seek some polite way of letting him know he was going too far. But if he rarely asks such favors, what do you really lose by saying yes?

Remember that your turn will come someday. If all goes well, you too will rise to high executive status. Then you can ask subordinates to do favors for *you*.

5. *Are you an innovator?*

It is not enough merely to become an expert in your job. Many people can do that, and most can at least become fast and efficient in carrying out job routines. What brings you to management's attention is the ability and willingness to reach out beyond routines. Keep asking: "Is there a better way?"

This requires that you keep your brain turned on all the time— a feat that most people seem to find difficult, though there is no good reason why it should be. Keep needling yourself: "Why am I doing it this way? Because my predecessor told me to? Did he learn it from *his* predecessor? Is it done this way because it's really the best way, or is it just a matter of bureaucratic habit?"

In the 1950s and 1960s, many companies formalized their need for bright new ideas by establishing highly publicized suggestion awards. If you were an employee with an innovative idea, you were invited to write it down and drop it in a suggestion box, and if your idea was adopted you received some kind of cash award, a testimonial dinner, and a handshake from the board chairman.

Suggestion boxes can still be seen here and there on plant and office walls, but there are no longer many companies that actively promote suggestion programs in the manner of the 1960s. The programs ran into all kinds of problems. There were disputes about the size of awards and the originality of ideas. In many companies the suggestion box turned into a repository for radical political manifestos, generalized gripes, and various kinds of unsigned obscenities. "The whole thing was more trouble than it was worth," says the personnel director of one company that long ago took down its suggestion boxes.

With boxes and formal programs dismantled, employees in many companies have seemed to get the feeling in recent years that their bright new ideas are no longer wanted.

This is definitely not true. The fact that something is not formally solicited doesn't mean it is not wanted.

Indeed, if your company has no active, formal program going, that very fact should spur you to greater alertness. For it means that not many people in the company will be actively trying to think of innovations and improvements. Anybody who does come forward with a useful new idea is going to be welcomed. The reward is likely to be considerably greater than a $250 check and a free dinner. The reward will be improved job security and increased chances of promotion.

One good way to develop innovations is to concentrate your attention on problems that crop up in your work. What is there that frustrates you? What doesn't seem to go right?

Most people, coming up against a problem, react by picking it up and taking it to a superior in its raw state: "Boss, we've got a problem." What *you* should do is go one step further. Go to your boss with the problem *and* a solution.

You may be able to find an innovative solution by brainstorming. This is a technique that has been a bit oversold in some business circles. It doesn't work at all for some men and women, and it works only intermittently for others. But it has been known to produce startlingly good results. The basic idea of it is to turn off your brain's critical function temporarily. Pondering a given problem, you list every solution that comes to mind, including silly and outlandish solutions. You deliberately avoid saying, "No, that's too goofy, it won't work."

For maybe it will work after all. This is the theory behind brainstorming. Most people criticize and discard their own good ideas too quickly. As a brainstormer you may conceive the same idea that has occurred to a lot of other people, but you will be the only one who thinks it all the way through.

Marie N. is one woman who had this experience. She worked out a way of color-coding customers' order forms so as to save enormous amounts of clerical time in a warehouse operation. "The idea came to me through brainstorming," she recalls. "I had this wacky idea of telling the customers to pay in Monopoly money—you know, with different denominations in different colors. That way we could tell at a glance how big the order was. I laughed at the notion, but then I thought, 'Wait a minute!' I went on thinking about color, and finally I arrived at a system that I thought could really be made to work. We tried it, and it did."

And Marie N. won a promotion not long afterward.

6. *Do you look as though you mean business?*

Grooming is important in the business world. That is a statement of plain fact. You may wish it were not so, and you may feel the unwritten rules of good grooming are silly. "After all," you say, "what counts is what goes on inside my head." Perhaps you are right. But if you want to argue the point, argue it with a friend in private. Don't assert it publicly by putting your job on the line.

For the fact is, whether we like it or not, grooming very definitely affects success and failure in business. For every nine people who love you for your inner self, there is always going to be one who objects to your careless grooming. That one person could be somebody with influence over your present and future security.

Remember, too, that people tend to make much more fuss about something wrong than something right. It's human nature. Customers are quick to take pen in hand when they are dissatisfied, but you don't often receive letters saying how nice everything is. And so it is with grooming. Well-groomed people don't get many direct compliments; they are taken for granted as part of the natural business environment. But ill-groomed people invite comment. "That fellow Jenkins," the chairman will say to the president, "do you suppose he never heard of shoe polish?"

Jenkins's job is not as secure as it might be.

Dress neatly, in the mode that is prevalent in your particular place of work. If the men are all in suits and the women in suits and dresses, then you had better attire yourself the same way. If more casual wear is prevalent, all right—but make sure you never let yourself get so casual that you cross the borderline into sloppiness. Try always to look clean and crisp, even if you wear blue jeans.

Perhaps it would be fun to be a maverick, but the fun is not worth the risk. You cannot afford it. You can be a clothing maverick only if you become so valuable to the company that you literally cannot be replaced.

Very few men or women ever reach such high standing, as was illustrated some years ago in a large international company. Until comparatively recent times, the grooming rule for male office workers in this company called for conservative suits, white shirts, and muted ties, all spanking clean and meticulously pressed. There was one man who disregarded these specifications and got away with it. He was a scientist of world repute. He habitually showed up for work in rumpled cord pants, a baggy tweed jacket, and shirts that looked as though they had been cut from potato sacks. Nobody said anything to him. He was the only one of his kind. He could not have been replaced at any price.

Two young physicists tried to copy him. They, too, wanted to announce their lofty intellectual status by ignoring the rules that applied to everybody else. Their rebellion did not last long. Their superior called them into his office and pointed out that the company could find a lot more young physicists where they came from. They were quite replaceable, he assured them.

A secure salary check is not something you give up lightly. The two young men instantly changed into conservative suits, white shirts, and muted ties.

It is also an excellent idea to pay attention to other aspects of the way you look. Cartoonists like to portray the typical successful business person as a cigar-smoking fat man, but the indications are that this is no longer an accurate reflection of real life, if it ever was. Today, successful business people are more likely to be those with lean, trim bodies. Several studies have demonstrated this. In one survey of fifteen thousand male executives, a distinct relationship was found between high income and a flat belly. The more overweight a man is, the study demonstrated, the lower his salary is likely to be.

A similar study of women in business was carried out by a University of California psychologist. She found a remarkable correlation between slimness and success. "In the upper executive offices of American business," she wrote, "fat women are almost as rare as they are on an Olympic track team."

The lesson is obvious. Pay attention not only to your clothes, but to your weight and other elements of your health. For if you are crisply groomed, if you stand erect, if you have a look of robust health and energy, then you look as though you mean business.

7. *Are you staying interested?*

An occasional boring day or even week is nothing to get alarmed about, but if you are a victim of chronic boredom, then something is wrong.

Job monotony is not only a symptom of things going wrong but a cause of further problems. As a symptom, it indicates that your job has become too much of a routine, with too little challenge and too little in the way of a future. This may or may not be your fault, but in any case you should do something about it. As a cause of trouble, job monotony leads you into a generalized slump. It always shows. You stop innovating; you stop showing any willingness to make extra effort; you may even lose interest in your appearance.

Don't just succumb to boredom. If it happens to you, don't just shrug and say, "This is what life is like behind a desk." It may be like that for some; perhaps it is for most—but it isn't supposed to be. When you feel boredom creeping up on you, treat it for what it is: an illness.

Assess the reasons behind it. Perhaps you are in a specialty that is becoming obsolete, or perhaps you are in a department or task group that your company is gradually abandoning. In such a case you should begin immediately to think about learning new skills and getting yourself transferred (see Chapter 8). Or perhaps the reasons lie inside yourself. You may simply have grown too comfortable in a daily routine, and what was once comfortable is now growing monotonous. Or you have neglected to see to your own continued education and growth; you have been doing the same thing too long; you need new worlds to conquer.

Continued education and training are excellent medicines against boredom. Look around; see what is being offered in your community. See what your company itself offers. Talk to your boss; find out if he or she has anything to suggest. As we've noted before, you score points by showing an eagerness for growth.

8. *Can you justify your salary?*

This is a question you should ask yourself often during your career. It is perhaps the most difficult question of all, for the answer is usually more than half subjective. It is a feeling: "Yes! I'm worth every nickel and then some!" If this feeling hits you strongly, that is a very good sign. But there are also some ways to get at the question objectively.

Some kinds of jobs can be evaluated financially more easily than others, of course—sales jobs, for example, or certain jobs that involve collecting money. Auditing agents of the Internal Revenue Service can justify their salaries partly on the basis of the amount of tax money they bring in each month.

But other jobs are less easy to measure in that way. Service-oriented and general management jobs command salaries that often seem to be arrived at arbitrarily. If you are in such a job, how do you know if you are genuinely earning what you get in that biweekly envelope?

There are two informal tests you can make:

□ Find out what others are getting in similar jobs—by checking help-wanted ads and by talking to people inside and outside your company. If you find your salary is within the prevalent range, then you can assume you are getting what the world considers a fair price for your work. If you find you are overpriced—which can happen because of too-long seniority or random dislocations such as a fit of corporate generosity in some long-vanished boom—then your job may be in jeopardy. In that case you had better go to work immediately to strengthen your position.

□ Listen to the feedback from upstairs. Do people ever compliment you on a job well done? This won't happen every week or every month, but does it happen at least sometimes? If they don't compliment you directly, do they do it indirectly by such means as asking your advice, asking you to take on special assignments, or making pleasant remarks about you to other people? (These remarks are likely to reach your ears in one way or another, for in all organizations there is a very lively kind of communication that is the opposite of malicious gossip. I've studied it, but few others have. It doesn't even have a name. Call it the good-news network. It springs from the fact that most people, on most days, enjoy being the bearers of good tidings.)

But beyond these objective and semiobjective tests, you will always come back to your own feeling about your job and paycheck. You know more about your job and your own performance than anybody else. If you aren't delivering, you aren't going to fool yourself. If you don't get that feeling—"I'm worth every nickel!"—then you should seriously ask yourself, "Why not?"

You can fool other people for a short time, but not forever.

3

Analyzing
the Organization

J ames Joseph Ling was a high-school dropout who began
his career as the owner of an obscure little electrical contracting business in Texas. He ended as the multimillionaire founder
of a giant conglomerate company now known as LTV. Musing about
his stunning success one day, he said he thought one of his most
valuable skills was the ability to understand organizations.

"I make a study of organizations," he said. "People tend to think
they're all pretty much alike—General Motors, Ford, Chrysler, what's
the difference. But the truth is they're as different as people are.
You can't be successful in dealing with any organization until you
understand it."

Ling was talking specifically about his problems as an equity
venturer studying organizations from the outside, but his words
apply cogently to any man or woman trying to deal with an organization from the inside. You, in other words. You are in this organization for better or worse. Your aim is to make your place in it more
secure. Your future depends on thoughts and actions that take place
in the hierarchies around and above you—including some thoughts
and actions of people you will never meet. To achieve security you

must clearly understand how this organization works and how its machinery impinges on you.

The Seat of Power

Nearly every business organization—including those that claim to operate by means of "team management"—has one man or woman at the apex of its power structure. This one person makes the final decisions on virtually all of the organization's large questions. I call this person the seat of power. All authority flows downward from this seat.

The seat of power is not necessarily the person with the grandest-sounding title. In some companies the most powerful person is the chairman of the board. In others, though the chairman may be named first in the annual report and may be portrayed with the biggest picture, the seat of power may be the president. This was the case for many years at NBC, for instance. The board chairman was Jane Cahill Pfeiffer, but the seat of power was the president, Fred Silverman. His day-to-day decisions, more than hers, affected the careers of those lower down in the power structure.

In still other companies, though more rarely, the seat of power may be the executive vice-president or somebody with another title. This happens most often in closely held or family-owned companies. The board chairman and president may both be major stockholders or family members who play only a distant role in the company's daily operations. The day-to-day operating decisions are made by a person who appears to rank third in terms of title but actually ranks first in terms of power.

In your attempt to understand the organization in which you work, your first step should be to locate the seat of power. Start by studying the latest annual report, if one is published. (It's surprising to me that many employees have never read their own companies' annual reports. Some reports are more informative than others, but you can usually find a lot of valuable clues to top management thinking among those glossy pages.) Read the report to see who is designated "chief executive officer." You can usually (but not always) assume that that person is the seat of power. Comb the report further to see who is mentioned most often as having decided this and decreed that. Meanwhile, listen to what is said around the company about the top management group. Who is talked about most often and with the greatest awe and respect?

═The Power Brokers═

Having located the seat of power, your next task is to map the lines of power as they reach down to your level. Between you and the top may be several levels of rank. Your boss reports, perhaps, to the controller, who reports to the vice-president in charge of finance, who reports to the president. The question you must ask yourself is: am I plugged in to a real hierarchy of power, or is it only a hierarchy of responsibility?

Every function in an organization carries responsibility, but not every function carries power.

There are people who talk with the seat of power and have influence there. There are others, of ostensibly equal rank, who do not. The people who have direct, influential contact with the seat of power, and the chains of people below who have influence on *them*, I call the power brokers.

To illustrate, let's suppose that in your company the seat of power is the president. The president is a man who holds an accounting degree, made his way up through the money-manipulating functions of management, and believes the way to keep the company afloat in today's stormy economic seas is sound finance. He listens closely to the advice of the financial vice-president, a woman of similar background and beliefs. She, therefore, is a power broker. To a lesser degree, so is the controller, who reports to and often confers closely with her; and to a still lesser degree, so is your boss, who has the ear and respect of the controller.

If this is your situation, you are in a basically promising job environment. You are directly plugged in to a line of power.

But let's suppose the situation is different. Let's say the president, the seat of power, is a marketing genius. Marketing has been his game throughout his career; it is the field in which he has made his name, and it is the reason why he has been installed as president. The directors pin their hopes on clever marketing strategy to pull the company through its difficulties, and he, of course, wholeheartedly shares that philosophy. Hence, he has lunch and plays golf often with the vice-president of marketing and the advertising director. *They* are the power brokers. The vice-president of finance, the controller, and your boss are not.

In this case you are in a vulnerable position. Your job is not as secure as you could wish. You are not in a department from which people are likely to be plucked for meaningful promotions. Thus, your indicated strategy would be either to seek ways of making your department more powerful or to get yourself transferred closer to the power brokers.

Neither of these two courses is exceptionally difficult, as we are going to see in forthcoming chapters. One man whose high climb I've studied started his career in an unpromising area: the personnel department of a large manufacturing company. Many companies respect and nurture their personnel departments, but in this particular company the president considered personnel an unimportant and even frivolous function. Indeed, it would not be an exaggeration to say he held it in contempt.

The man I'm talking about—call him Ed—observed this distressing fact soon after being hired into the personnel department. Carefully examining the company's power structure in the ways I've indicated, he saw that the main power brokers were the finance and engineering people. They had the president's ear. Their departments were lavishly rewarded with money; their people were secure in their jobs and were routinely promoted up the ladder.

The personnel department, by contrast, was a Siberia. People froze there. The personnel director was rarely invited to the really important deliberations in the upper executive offices. He was not in any sense a power broker; nor was Ed's immediate superior, the supervisor of benefit programs, who reported to the personnel director.

Ed concluded that his only feasible route to security and promotions was to get into either the finance or the engineering operations of the company. He knew virtually nothing of engineering but had had considerable financial schooling and felt capable of learning more on the subject quickly. He prescribed a course of study for himself, bided his time, kept his eyes and ears open.

His chance soon came. His group was given the task of streamlining the company's poorly organized benefits program. He volunteered to make an analysis of costs. When he was satisfied that the analysis was the best piece of work he could do, he showed it to the controller, who had asked to be consulted about it. The controller was impressed with Ed's clear, concise presentation. The chemistry between the two men was good. Without saying anything unkind about the personnel department, Ed managed to make known his desire to get into financial-analysis work. In time, the controller had him transferred.

Ed today is a member of that company's top management team. He himself is one of the power brokers. He has tried to do things for the friends he left behind in the personnel department, but the company president's feelings about it have not changed. Most of those working in that department still have dim futures, at best.

It is sad that perfectly good people so often languish in inactive departments with poor leadership. I've watched them: impressively bright people, some of them, doomed to spend years of their lives turning out reams of reports that nobody will ever read. In good times they may get token raises because the corporation feels charitable. In less than good times their salaries are the first to be frozen, and they are first on the list of expendable employees who can be dumped if necessary. That is a fate to be avoided.

═Identifying the Power Brokers═

In some companies it is fairly easy to identify the power brokers, in others not so easy. Here are the main clues to look for:

□ *Power brokers are talked about.* Listen to what is said not only by people at your own level of rank, but also by those above you. Listen to what your boss says on the phone. Listen in elevators, at meetings. The names of power brokers tend to come up often, and there will frequently be a tone of awe or anxiety in the speaker's voice: "I don't know what Mr. Walters is going to say when he hears about this . . ."

□ *Access to these powerful people is seldom easy.* There may be a lot of pious talk around the company about easy access. "My door is always open to anybody with a problem," the president will say in his best avuncular voice, and other executives will parrot the statement. In practice, however, it is usually a sham. Access to the least powerful may be easy enough. But if you have a problem that needs the attention of a power broker, first you talk to his secretary, and if you are lucky she will then pass you through to his assistant.

□ *As a general rule, you can guess who at least some of the power brokers are by reading up on the background of the top person, the seat of power.* This background may be alluded to in an annual report or may be sketched in a magazine article—or may simply be common knowledge throughout the company. The top person will usually lean toward those of similar background; they will be the power brokers.

At Polaroid Corp., for instance, the seat of power for years was the founder and president, Edwin Land. A scientist, Land naturally elevated research-oriented people to high positions in his stunningly successful company. Research and engineering groups were good places to be.

However, don't make the mistake of supposing these people sharing the top person's background are the only power brokers. Edwin Land always had enormous respect for the marketing function, though he admitted it was not his own area of expertise. Hence, marketing people at Polaroid were also well plugged in to lines of power.

Conversely, marketing has almost always been the main interest of the seat of power at Procter & Gamble. The company's last three chairmen—John Hanley, Howard Morgens, and Edward Harness—all came up through fields such as marketing, advertising, and promotion, and naturally the strongest lines of power in that company have been the lines that went through those departments. But Harness, for one, has put heavy emphasis on research and testing—

particularly since the company's Rely-brand tampons got involved in a staggeringly expensive medical scare in 1980. Thus, if you work in or around a lab at P&G, the chances are you are plugged in to power.

□ *Power brokers have perks, often highly visible.* Look for the men and women with big offices, the ones who are privileged to ride in the company plane. "At our company," says a woman who works for a Connecticut-based insurance company, "we can tell who has the power partly by looking at the reserved spaces in the parking lot. The president and chairman get to park closest to the building. Then come others in descending order of power, more or less. But you have to read it carefully. There's at least one man who is near retirement and has hardly any power or even any function anymore, but he has a close-in parking space because he's been around longer than anybody else."

All clues about power brokers must be read with care, in fact. Don't depend on only one clue or two. Investigate thoroughly in all the ways I've outlined, and don't stop investigating until you have a solid package of clues that all seem to agree. When you have all those clues assembled, you will know whether you are close enough to the power.

4

Who Is Your Boss?

Tom Watson, Sr., the founding genius and first president of IBM, remarked once that four people stood out in his mind as having influenced his life more profoundly than any others. "Those four," he said, "were my two parents, a certain teacher, and my first boss." He paused, then added, "And I didn't necessarily name them in order of importance."

It may never have occurred to you that your immediate superior—your boss—might turn out to be as important a figure in your life as a parent or a favorite teacher. But consider the enormous power that lies in this man's or woman's hands. Your boss may have hired you and probably has power to fire you, or at least to see to it that somebody else does. He or she can smooth your road toward raises and promotions—or, conversely, can put obstacles in your path, hold you back, and make your life miserable. Your boss can teach you, guide you, show you vistas of career exploration that you might never have seen on your own—or, conversely, can squeeze you, cramp you, make you so discontented that you become nothing but a time-server, the first to be fired when conditions are bad, lacking any future even if business is good.

46

Considering the staggering importance of a boss, it often surprises me to see how casually most people approach the boss-subordinate relationship. The prevailing view seems to be that this relationship is something that comes into being by itself, and you simply have to take what you get. In other words: depend on luck.

If you hold that view, you could be heading for career disaster. Your relationship with your immediate superior should *not* be left to chance. If you want to make your present position secure and build solid hopes for the future, it is essential that you study this powerful person with care and interface with him or her *methodically*.

If, by luck, the relationship has started out well and seems to be based solidly on mutual liking and respect, then you have a good foundation to build on. This doesn't mean you can sit back and take the happy circumstance for granted. The seemingly strong bonds between you and your affable boss could be ripped to shreds in some unforeseeable crisis in the future. What you must do is work to understand the relationship. Know how you will preserve it and protect yourself if and when that crisis arises.

If the relationship is poor—or, just as bad, if you don't know exactly *where* you stand with your boss—then the need for work is more acute. Your job is not as secure as it ought to be. You have left too much to chance.

Whatever you do, don't give in to frustration, lose your temper, and leave the job. I've known many people to quit their jobs in a sudden fit of anger or disgust, and the most commonly given reason is "I couldn't get along with my boss." Certainly, it is normal and human to get frustrated with a bad situation that fails to improve itself, but walking off the job is the very, very last solution you should think of. It is almost always better to stick with what you've got and try to improve it.

I would give this advice even in the best of economic times. In less-than-boom times such as the present, the advice takes on a sharper edge. If you quit your job, you are not going to find a lot of other prospective bosses knocking at your door to offer you a new one.

═Who Is Your Boss? ═══════════

Start by making a close study of this man or woman, your boss. Find out as much as you can. Some information about him or her will undoubtedly be open and public; some will be partially hidden, discoverable only by listening to the grapevine and observing your boss in day-to-day interactions with other people.

The point of this study is that your own fate is linked with your superior's. If this boss of yours is considered a comer, is marked for bigger things, is granted power and decision-making leeway, then he or she can give you various kinds of highly valuable help with your career. Indeed, if the relationship is strong enough, your boss can even become your mentor (Chapter 5). But if your boss lacks power, is considered to be dead-ended, or is on the way out, then you can expect little help or solid support from this source no matter how fond the relationship may be—and, that being the case, will have to seek your security in other ways.

Find out first where your department fits in the corporate scheme. What is its relationship to other departments? Is it considered important, or are there some who consider it a joke? Does it seem to get its fair share of budgeted money?

"I found out where my boss and my department really stood when I started to pay attention to expense-account rules," recalls a woman who used to work for an electronics company. "I thought my department was about average in terms of importance until I had lunch one day with a friend from another department and we compared notes on business trips we'd taken recently. I complained about the stringent rules we had to follow: we could charge meals to expenses only under certain conditions, and we were allowed to spend only so much, and we had to get receipts for everything, including two-dollar cab rides. My friend looked surprised and said nobody had ever imposed those rules on her. She was allowed to charge whatever she felt was reasonable. Well, this was a revelation to me. I'd thought all departments had penny-pinching budgets. Now I began to see that my boss wasn't one of the company's fair-haired boys. The department was a dead end, in fact. I worked hard to get myself moved out of it."

Watch for clues as that woman did. Listen to what people say about your department. Don't put too much faith in what people tell you or what you have observed about other companies. *This* company is the one that counts. In some organizations the personnel department is among the first to be chopped in hard times, while in others—IBM is an example—it is a department of high status and considerable power.

If you determine that your department holds low rank or is a dead end, that will be a signal that you should study your boss with extra care. It may turn out that you have little to worry about; perhaps he or she is a strong leader who was assigned to this loser department for the specific purpose of improving its fortunes. In that case, stand hard by; you could have a good future. On the other hand, maybe the reverse is true: your boss was assigned to the department when it was strong but then allowed it to collapse. Or—a third possibility—this boss of yours is somebody who failed in another department and was dumped into this one because nobody considers it important.

If either of the last two possibilities is true, you have two choices. Either you should seek to get transferred out of the department, or you should work to help your boss strengthen it. We will discuss both kinds of strategy in due course.

Though many of your clues about your boss will come from the company grapevine, you can also get a wealth of information by studying him or her at first hand. Some of your best clues will come (if you are alert) from situations of sudden surprise. Watch how your boss reacts, for example, when a secretary comes in with some bad news, or when a superior phones and unexpectedly moves up a deadline for completion of a project.

In my experience, observing somebody interacting with a superior is probably the very best way of arriving at judgments about that person's standing, power, confidence, and competence. There are three main categories of reaction to a sudden, distressing phone call from a superior:

1. *Calm and confident:* "Sure, Paul, we can speed up the work on this project. It'll mean rescheduling some other work, but nothing we can't handle. Tuesday? No, I'm afraid that would be cutting it too close. We wouldn't have time to check our work the way we like. What would you say to Wednesday? . . . Yes, that is a promise."

A conversation like that gives you a lot of encouraging information about your boss. This man or woman is confident of his or her ability to lead the department and organize its work, confident of the team's capacity to perform well under stress. The conversation shows also that your boss is well thought of in the upper executive offices—is secure enough to stand fast when a superior makes an unreasonable demand. Moreover, your boss has the skill to disagree with a superior in such a way as to gain rather than lose credit from the exchange. The superior, though blocked in his wish to have the project finished by Tuesday, might well have put down the phone and said, "That fellow really seems to know what he's doing."

2. *Overeager:* "Sure, Paul! Of course! I'll get on it right away! No problem, no problem! Right! You bet!"

This boss seems too anxious to please. Insecurity comes through the words. You can be doubly sure of this judgment if you discover, over a period of time, that your boss often makes promises that cannot be kept—promises, for example, about project deadlines that your department is incapable of meeting.

3. *Panicky:* "Tuesday? Oh my God, that's—well, I'll see if I can find—I don't know if—you wouldn't believe how much pressure we've—listen, can I call you back? . . ."

This sounds very much like a boss who not only lacks a sense of confidence and security, but feels the ground slipping away like loose sand underfoot.

As I've said, you can elect either to get out from under or to stick around and make improvements if you determine that your boss is a person in trouble. But you have already taken the supremely important first step: you have gone to the trouble of finding out who your boss is and where he stands. Most people don't take even that elementary precaution.

⸻*Cultivating a Good Relationship*⸻

Some bosses, of course, are easier to get along with than others. Some are intimidatingly difficult. I know of one man who, through a series of flukes, was promoted far beyond his level of competence and found himself floundering. His department was a shambles; its work was chronically late and slipshod; other departments that depended on that work were complaining more and more loudly. This man's response was to put all the blame on his subordinates. "They let me down," he would say. "We gave them a chance to show what they could do and they blew it."

A difficult situation indeed. Two of his subordinates got themselves transferred out of the department, one through the intervention of a mentor. Another group took the opposite tack: they analyzed the department's problems and tactfully suggested ways in which the boss could bring its performance up to par. They let him take most of the credit but made sure some of it rubbed off on them.

The only people who got hurt in this situation were those who did nothing. There were a few who simply sat, allowing themselves to be associated with the department's former state of disarray. Two or three lost their jobs in one of the "austerity" programs that the company periodically launched to hold up its sagging earnings, while the others, when I last heard of them, still had their jobs but seemed to be going nowhere. All these do-nothing people had their careers seriously set back.

Few bosses are that difficult, fortunately. As a general rule—with exceptions—people who rise to leadership positions in business are men and women who have learned how to conduct themselves in a courteous, businesslike, professional way. Thus, statistically, you are probably going to meet more capable and likable bosses in your career than difficult ones.

But even the most forthright, amiable, considerate, and confident boss needs careful cultivating. Just as it is seldom a good idea to lie down and quit in a bad situation, so it is hazardous to take a good situation for granted.

Here are the most important points to bear in mind in your approach to your boss:

Be supportive. You've found out what your boss's standing is, what his or her problems are, what he or she wants. Now you must figure out how you can help your boss get what he or she wants.

Be very careful in all your attempts to help. Be sure your actions not only *are* supportive but look that way to your boss. Different bosses will react in different ways, for example, to a subordinate who offers to take over a few new responsibilities. One boss may be glad to get rid of some headaches; another may think the subordinate is a busybody; a third may feel threatened by what looks like an attempt to move in on his or her territory.

To avoid bad outcomes, assess your boss. If he or she seems insecure, move very, very slowly in your attempts to help. An insecure boss feels threats from all directions.

Also be aware of your own attitude and the signals you are sending. Your attitude should not say, "Boss, I want your job." Instead, it should say, "If you succeed, boss, I succeed. I want to help you make a good name for yourself."

Be supportive no matter what happens. There may come a time, for instance, when you feel you know more about a certain situation than your boss does. This is a common occurrence, particularly with the kind of boss who habitually delegates tasks to subordinates and lets them work out their own approaches. If you have spent an entire week working on a certain problem, it is perfectly conceivable that by Friday you will know considerably more about it than your boss does.

That being so, it is also conceivable that your boss will make suggestions or ask questions based on inadequate knowledge. Now is the time to remember the rule: be supportive. Your boss's suggestion may be utterly ridiculous, but you must be careful not to say that or imply it in your words, looks, or attitude. Instead, find a way to set the facts straight without making your boss feel foolish: "Yes, the same idea occurred to me, but it turns out there's a catch . . ." And then find a way to reassure your boss that he or she *is* the boss. One excellent way is to ask for guidance: "Since there's no way around the problem, I'm at a loss about what to do. What do you think?"

Tell your boss what you are doing. This is especially important if your boss feels less than perfectly secure. An insecure person is always wondering what people are doing and saying when out of sight, and will constantly imagine dark plots and conspiracies. Protect yourself against these fear-ridden imaginings by being candid about all the important events of your office life.

This doesn't mean you should report trivia to your boss—and you should certainly *not* report on other people like a KGB spy. What it means is that you should find seemingly casual ways to let your boss know of your own moves. If you've had lunch with a friend from another department or a talk with a senior executive, mention these facts casually when you get the chance.

It may seem silly, but it is better to tell your boss about some encounter than to have him or her find out about it by chance from somebody else. For this is how the fearful imaginings get their start: why was so-and-so talking to the vice-president? Why wasn't I told? Were they discussing something they don't want me to know about?

When your boss begins to think thoughts like these, you are probably in trouble.

Let your boss win arguments. Understand how much the average person hates to lose an argument with a subordinate. It may be necessary for you to swallow your pride once in a while. If it is necessary, do it and try to forget it.

Try to end every confrontation on a positive note, even if it does hurt your pride: "Yes, you're right, I shouldn't have handled it that way..." You walk out of your boss's office feeling put-upon and angry, perhaps—but look at it this way: your principal mission is to preserve your job and get promoted, not win arguments. A certain amount of swallowed pride and suppressed anger isn't that great a price to pay. The bad feeling won't last long. Tomorrow the air will have cleared.

Never, never storm out of your boss's office with angry words and a slammed door. Nor is it ever a good idea to let a confrontation end inconclusively: "Well, I'll think about it." All that does is keep the disagreement simmering. It may evaporate, but don't count on that. The best strategy is to find a positive ending and get it over with.

If you must correct your boss's facts, do it gently. Though you will usually want to let your boss win arguments—particularly arguments having to do with questions of opinion—there will be times when your boss plainly and simply has the facts wrong. If the consequences of this are trivial, let it go; say nothing. But if you judge that the consequences could be severe, to you personally or to the department's work, then you will have to speak up. But remember my warning against doing or saying things that your boss could feel as threats. Don't correct those faulty facts in such a way as to make your boss look foolish, and don't do it angrily, even though your boss's mistake could have cost you dearly.

Let's suppose your boss calls you in one day and says: "I think it's time you and I had a little talk about the working hours around here. This company pays you a damned good salary, and in return we expect five honest days of work from you every week. I've been watching you, and it seems to me you've been getting to work later every morning. Why, I don't think you've gotten to your desk any earlier than ten this whole week . . ."

Your boss has the facts wrong. The truth is that you've been working on a project requiring library research. You've been spending the first two hours each morning in the company library.

You've got to say something. Those faulty facts could do serious damage to your job security and your career. What do you do?

Don't make your boss look like a jackass: "Maybe one day you'll bother to get your facts straight before you go around throwing accusations at people . . ."

Don't get angry: "This really takes the cake! You owe me an apology! . . ."

Instead, tell your boss that a perfectly understandable mistake has been made—a mistake that any smart person would be likely to make in the same circumstances—and then state the correct facts in a straightforward and unemotional way. Smilingly say, "Oh, yes, it's my fault, really. I should have told you what I've been up to. How could you be expected to know? You see, I've been working in the library every morning . . ."

Be interested in your boss's personal life. Not all men and women care to communicate personal trivia to subordinates, but the majority do. I'm not quite sure why this is so. Perhaps it springs from a boss's wish to seem human. "You see, I'm a flesh-and-blood person just like you," the boss seems to be saying. "I've got a family, I've got likes and dislikes, I've got problems like anybody else. I'm really a pretty lovable person, don't you see that?"

Most bosses want to be liked. If yours does, cooperate.

Be interested when your boss talks about his or her kids and spouse—and for goodness' sake remember their names. Try to remember other personal details too. It will please and flatter your boss if, months after you hear some trivial detail, you show that it has stuck in your mind: "You once told me you're fond of those hero sandwiches they make at the deli across the street. Why don't I pick up a couple for us to eat on the road?"

Conversely, failure to remember a personal detail could lower you in your boss's esteem. An executive recalls a time when, as a younger man, he worked under a woman boss. She was a recovered alcoholic and a member of Alcoholics Anonymous. Members of AA are encouraged to talk openly of their problem—or at least not to make any attempt to hide it. "My boss didn't talk about it often," the man recalls, "but at a sales dinner one night, when the rest of us were having drinks and she wasn't, she did mention alcoholism in an offhand way. I remembered this, but apparently not everyone else was as careful about personal details as I was."

The man was promoted out of the woman boss's department shortly after that sales dinner. A month or so later he had lunch with a younger man who was making a good name for himself in her department and hoped soon to be promoted as her second-in-command.

"It's the personal touch that gets you ahead," the younger man said, sounding pleased with himself. "She won a management award last week, so a few of us chipped in and got her a gift. We left it on her desk. She'll be finding it just about now as she gets back from lunch."

"Oh? What did you get her?"

"A bottle of champagne."

The inattentive young man never became the woman's second-in-command. He marked time for two years, got impatient, quit, and was never heard of around that company again.

You may be thoroughly bored by your boss's revelations about his or her Siamese cat, favorite restaurant, or golf score. But you had better listen alertly and with at least an appearance of interest.

═Handling a Change in Your Boss═

A sudden, unexplained change in a boss can be bewildering and frightening for subordinates. Your boss used to be amiable; now, abruptly, he or she seems distant, unfriendly, unnecessarily brusque. What should you do?

The first thing to do is wait a few days. Perhaps the change is caused by some passing problem having nothing to do with you. Don't overreact to just one instance of abrupt or rude behavior on your boss's part. We all have our bad days.

But if the changed behavior continues or gets worse, carefully observe what is going on. Is this new behavior general? That is, does your boss behave in this changed manner with everybody? Or does the abruptness seem to be directed only at you?

If it seems directed at everybody, listen to the grapevine and see if you can find out what has caused the change. It may be that a crisis is coming, and you will need to protect yourself. Or perhaps whatever has gone wrong is something you can help with. Remember the importance of supporting your boss when you can.

If the unfriendly behavior seems aimed at you alone, then it is time for you to have a talk with your boss. Be pleasant and unemotional: "We've always had a good relationship, but something seems to have happened. Is something wrong? I'd like to straighten it out if I can."

This may be just the opening your boss has been waiting and hoping for. Perhaps he or she does have a genuine complaint against you. You may have made a mistake without realizing it. Or perhaps somebody has misreported something you've done or said. At any rate, your boss has been angered, has wanted to air the problem with you, but has kept putting the moment off. This kind of procrastination is altogether human. Nobody likes unpleasant scenes; very few people look forward to chastising a subordinate. Indeed, parents even procrastinate before confronting a child or teenager over some developing problem.

Thus, your boss may react with a feeling of great relief when you voluntarily initiate the dreaded confrontation. You are likely to hear your boss say, "Why, yes, there *has* been something I've wanted to talk to you about . . . Why don't you sit down . . . ?"

And while your boss walks across the office to shut the door, you will have some moments to collect yourself and remind yourself of our major rule about confrontations with one's boss: whatever the coming unpleasantness is to be about, let your boss win.

When it is over, the air will have begun to clear. With any kind of luck, you and your boss can then reestablish your relationship as it was before.

But what if your boss doesn't take you up on your offer to get the problem aired and disposed of? Suppose you ask what is wrong and your boss only mumbles, "Nothing," or "Nothing to do with you," or "Wrong? Nothing's wrong. You're imagining things!"

In that case, drop it. Don't needle your boss or come back whining: "I *know* something's wrong! You just don't behave the way you used to around me!" As a general rule, somebody who has decided to hide a problem cannot be talked into revealing it. I've seen this happen so rarely that I'm tempted to say it just about never happens. Your boss's reasons for ducking a confrontation over the problem may be sound or not, may be smart or may be dumb, but they are reasons that probably are not going to be budged.

Instead of badgering your boss about this, put your ear to the grapevine. Listen to what others are saying. Think back over your own activities in recent days and weeks. If you can pinpoint the day or week when you first noticed your boss's changed behavior, focus on what you were doing that day or week. This could give you the clues you need to explain what is troubling your boss and what you should do about it.

═Handling a New Boss ═

The time when a new boss is moved in over your head is among the more hazardous periods in anybody's working career. This is the time when you must be ready for the "deck-clearing" operation that almost any new superior is likely to launch. At its mildest, such an operation will involve changing certain rules and procedures; in a more severe form it will mean some changes in the relative status and power of various people in the department; and at its worst it will involve the dreaded game of "cleaning out deadwood"—meaning that some will be demoted or fired. Whether it is mild or severe, you must prepare yourself for it.

When you get a new job and start work under an established boss, that boss usually gives you some kind of personal orientation. Though perhaps inadequate, such an orientation is at least a well-meant attempt to start a working relationship on the right foot. But when the situation is reversed—when the boss is the departmental newcomer and the subordinates are the old-timers—such attempts at personal relationship-making are rare, in my observation. What most often happens is that the new chief calls the whole department together for some kind of orientation and pep talk, before or after which the chief may have some private sessions with one or two of the top staffers. Most of the new boss-subordinate relationships, however, are left to develop on a basis of chance and hope.

Don't let that happen to you.

What you must do, soon after a new chief gets installed, is *take the first step* in getting a good relationship established. Don't sit around and hope the new leader will take the initiative. Instead, get yourself into this unknown newcomer's office without delay. Announce your wish to be supportive: "I thought you'd like a rundown on what I'm involved in . . . I want to be sure I understand your thinking thoroughly . . ."

Three strong hints:

□ *Don't play the role of wise old counselor offering a helping hand to the new kid on the block.* Avoid phraseology such as "I'll be happy to give you some guidance" or "I'll show you the ropes." You may, in fact, be offering some such service, but it would be a mistake to say so. Remember that, though you may be a departmental old-timer, you are still a subordinate.

□ *Don't betray excessive nostalgia for your former, departed boss.* "It's a shame Jack had to leave," says an unwise subordinate, "we really have had a terrific team going here. I hope the old spirit stays alive . . ." Yes, you do want to speak in pleasant terms of the departed chief; and yes, you do want to show that you are a dedicated member of the team. But carefully avoid making your new chief feel like an intruder who has blundered into a private party of old friends. Rather, your aim should be to make the new team leader feel welcome. If you want to talk about the old team spirit, say something like: "I think you're going to enjoy leading this group. You'll find we work together well, and we're eager to know what new adventures you have in mind for us . . ."

☐ *Obey whatever new rules your new chief may establish, no matter how silly and trivial they may seem.* As I remarked before, an incoming new leader almost always likes to make changes of some kind. The changes may be severe, or they may be merely symbolic, designed simply to establish the new source of authority and underline the fact that leadership has changed. Your new boss's new rules may have to do with matters such as the time allowed for coffee breaks or the proper method of entering car mileage on expense accounts. Perhaps you and all the other departmental veterans are certain the new rules won't work, or perhaps you simply consider them too silly to be taken seriously. No matter. Obey them anyway. Your new boss must be granted the prerogative of making symbolic changes in rules. Be thankful if they are only small and symbolic.

If they really don't work, that fact may become self-evident in time and they will be rescinded. If they aren't and if they remain truly irksome, wait until your relationship with the new chief is solidly established before doing anything. The worst thing you can do is to start griping about changes before the new boss has come to know you. If you do that, you get yourself marked with some labels you can do without: "Troublemaker . . . not a team player . . . can't live with rules."

═Entertainment and Gifts═

The boss-subordinate relationship seems to generate a lot of clichés. One of the oldest is the situation in which a subordinate invites a boss home for dinner. I don't know how many TV sitcoms I've watched on this subject.

I must tell you, however, that in real life it is becoming less and less common. George Bellamy, a recently retired General Electric employee, recalls that "inviting the boss home" was a yearly ritual when he started the long climb after World War II. "My wife and I just plain assumed it was part of the job," he says. "So did all the other young couples in our social circle. Once a year or so you invited your boss home for a great gourmet meal. It was always a quite uncomfortable meal, as I recall. I'm sure the boss would just as soon have skipped it too. I was glad to see the custom start to die out in the 1970s."

My advice today: don't make a big deal out of entertaining your boss. If an occasion arises naturally, all right. If, for example, you and your boss are taking off on a trip together and you need to stop at your home to pick up something, then you can easily and naturally suggest that your boss come in for a meal or a drink. Or if you and your boss are waiting for a delayed flight together at an airport, you can offer to buy a couple of beers or some coffee. That is no more than ordinary human hospitality. But to plan a five-course dinner is a different matter. Unless you have known your boss for a long, long time and feel you are more than usually friendly, don't plan any such special entertainments.

Leave the office to the office.

I would also counsel you, in general, to avoid giving your boss Christmas or birthday gifts. You will only make the man or woman uncomfortable. In all my observations of the career scene, I have never seen a case in which a subordinate bought a boss's favor by showering him or her with merchandise.

Like any human, however, a boss does feel flattered when somebody pays attention on a special day. I once saw a very adroit move by a young woman in this respect. She had decided that it would be inappropriate to give her boss a personal birthday gift, but she thought he might appreciate something inexpensive from the department as a group. She therefore went to the boss's secretary and asked when the man's birthday was.

The secretary provided the information, then mentioned this

conversation to the boss. This was exactly what the young woman had hoped would happen. The boss was secretly pleased and flattered by her attentiveness. When the departmental birthday party was held, she got the credit for it.

5

The Essential Mentor

Read some biographies of men and women who rose high in the world of business and you will find a common thread running through most of their stories. People like Helena Rubinstein, the cosmetics queen; Lee Iacocca, the man who saved Chrysler; Peter Cohen, the young president of Shearson/American Express: all had a certain kind of help in their careers. Each, at an early stage of the long climb, was adopted by a mentor.

It is essential that you thoroughly understand this familiar but seemingly mysterious figure in the job world, the mentor. Everybody needs a mentor—not just the people at the top, not just those who make a big splash and become the subjects of biographies, but every man and woman who holds a white-collar job.

Your mentor, if you have one and if he or she is the right one for you, can easily double your job security. This comforting and protecting person can keep you on the payroll when others around you are being thrown overboard willy-nilly. On a more positive note, your mentor can also open your path to raises and promotions—and that, after all, is the best kind of job security.

My studies of the career scene have convinced me that most employed men and women have only vague and often faulty notions about mentors. Some have mentors. Some don't. Some think they might have but aren't sure. Most assume that a mentor is heaven-sent; you get one if fate is on your side, and if you don't get one, there is nothing you can do about it. It is the purpose of this chapter to show you that, in this respect, your fate is actually in your own hands.

You need a mentor. You must have one. You can acquire one through your own efforts.

══*What Is a Mentor?* ═══════════

There are two main elements in my definition of a mentor. If somebody does not display these two characteristics clearly and unequivocally, that person is not a true mentor—and, as we will see later, should be approached with caution. The definitions:

1. A mentor is a man or woman who has a *genuine* fondness for and interest in a lower-ranking, less experienced employee. Notice that word *genuine*. We will come back to it.

2. A mentor is a man or woman who holds a position of power in the organization. He or she isn't necessarily one of the organization's major power brokers, nor necessarily a member of the top brass. This part of the definition means only that the mentor has enough power to exert tangible influence on the protégé's career.

If you have identified someone as a possible mentor and these two characteristics don't shine through strongly, be careful. You could be starting along a false trail, and the mistake could be costly.

I once studied the career of a woman executive who had made such a mistake. Early in her career, as a new employee in a large New York bank, she was one of a dozen young men and women selected for special training and grooming. All were deemed to have the potential to move, in time, into important decision-making jobs. The opportunity pleased her but also frightened her, for she realized there was a price to pay for this special treatment. The price was special scrutiny: her performance would be watched and analyzed with more than usual care.

Thus, she was relieved and comforted when an apparent mentor appeared on the scene. This was an older woman with the title of assistant vice-president. The young woman's duties took her regularly into the offices of people at that managerial level. She and the older woman developed what looked like a mentor-protégé relationship very rapidly. "Why don't we have a drink together after work?" the older woman would suggest. "Maybe I can give you some pointers . . ."

It seemed like a lucky break, an ideal turn of events for any jobholder with fears for the present and hopes for the future. What the young woman failed to perceive, however, was that the older woman lacked both key characteristics of a true mentor.

In the first place, she did not possess power to any substantial degree. The younger woman was fooled partly by that grand-sounding title, assistant vice-president; it made the holder sound like a much bigger fish than she really was. Banks often bestow such titles, as do other organizations that deal personally with large numbers of clients. The title is designed more to impress clients than to serve as an accurate indicator of rank, prestige, and power.

In the second place, the older woman's interest did not spring from motives of genuine fondness or an honest wish to be helpful. Rather, her main motive was to use the younger woman as a spy. The older woman wanted to know what certain other assistant vice-presidents were up to. She and they—a group of five or six—were all tacitly felt to be in line for a bigger job that was soon to be created in the bank's trust department. The new job was viewed as a particularly juicy plum, and a good deal of secret maneuvering and dark-corner whispering was afoot.

The episode ended badly for the young woman. The coveted job eventually went to a man—one of the assistant vice-presidents on whom she had been spying for the woman she thought was her mentor. The man had become aware of the spying toward the end of the contest, had been at first annoyed and finally enraged by it, and had resolved to avenge himself if he ever got the chance. He was an extremely vengeful man. His new job gave him new power. Nothing was ever said directly, but the young woman slowly came to understand that she had been dropped from the special fast-track group. She remained dead-ended for years.

Her supposed mentor neither had the power to protect her nor gave a damn.

══*A Mentor's Motives*══════════

We get back to that word *genuine*. If you understand what motivates a true mentor, you will be in a better position to tell the true from the false.

One element of motivation is the ordinary, selfless wish of the veteran to help the rookie—the same motive that makes a teacher want to help a student, makes a mother counsel a bride, makes neighbors drop in to welcome a newcomer. If *selfless* is too sentimental a word for your taste, all right, call it simply friendly. Perhaps there is a certain amount of self-interest involved. People undoubtedly behave in this generous way because it makes them feel good; it gives them a feeling of importance; it advertises the scope of their experience. On the other hand, don't make the mistake of being too cynical about this universal human act. We like helping those of less experience because . . . well, just because that is the way humans are made.

Another important element of motivation, no doubt, is a kind of mirror effect. The mentor sees his or her earlier self in the protégé. As the protégé advances along the upward path of a career, the mentor can derive vicarious enjoyment from the process.

Various kinds of overt self-interest may also be involved. The mentor may be in the process of building an empire and seeking trustworthy allies, for example. Or perhaps the mentor feels overloaded with responsibilities or problems and needs a helper who is more than just a paid assistant. Such self-interested motives exist compatibly with the purely generous motives in a true mentor. It is only when the selfish motives dominate the relationship—as in the case of the woman bank officer—that the supposed mentor must be suspected of being false.

══*The Many Kinds of Mentor*══════════

As you start looking around for a potential mentor, it will be essential that you make your field of search broad enough. Don't make the very common mistake of narrowing it by looking for only one kind of mentor. There are, in fact, many kinds. If you pass over some of the less easily recognized kinds in your search, you could be missing valuable opportunities. The four main kinds of mentor are:

THE PARENT FIGURE   This is the classic mentor, the most easily recognized, the kind most people would describe if you asked them what a mentor is. The Parent Figure is the venerable, gray-haired, battle-seasoned man or woman who adopts a protégé young enough to be a son or daughter.

THE WHIZ KID   This mentor may be only slightly older than the protégé but is, of course, senior in experience and power. He or she is a fast-track climber, typically a business-school graduate, very often somebody who scored brilliant career successes at an unusually early age. Don't overlook this person in your search. A large difference in age is by no means necessary to a pleasant and productive mentor relationship.

THE LEANING MENTOR   This person is often brilliant in his or her central areas of interest but lacks competence in other areas. Instinctively feeling this lack, the mentor adopts a protégé who is able and willing to supply the missing talents. Howard Hughes, for instance, a brilliant and imaginative business strategist, had scant patience for the day-to-day demands of business life and never learned how to deal with people effectively in situations of stress. He knew this. Hence, early in his astonishing career he adopted young Noah Dietrich as a protégé, and he leaned on Dietrich ever more heavily as the two of them moved from one success to another.

THE FALSE MENTOR   As we have seen, this is the person who looks and acts like a mentor but is not. Becoming entangled with such a person won't necessarily do you great damage; you can learn from somebody who lacks power, for example, and perhaps you can make a friend. But even if the relationship has these benign results, it is essential that you recognize it for what it is: something other than a true mentor relationship. Don't be lulled. You still lack a true mentor and, lacking one, are not as secure in your job as you could be.

In searching for your mentor you need not confine yourself narrowly to your own department. Your best mentor may turn out to be your immediate boss, or somebody else who is directly in line with your particular function. If so, that can make it easy; you are or can be in regular contact with this person and may not need to try too hard to establish a mentor relationship. But if you are not so lucky, look beyond your immediate office neighborhood. As we will see, there are ways to make contact with a potential mentor even though he or she is fairly far from your place in the organizational scheme.

Nor need you restrict yourself to people of your own sex. Until comparatively recent times, the great majority of mentor-protégé pairs in most industries were of the same sex—male. This, of course, came about because most positions of power in most businesses were held by men. It was quite rare that a man in a power position would think of grooming a woman for eventual executive status. Today, however, changes are happening rapidly. More and more women are rising into decision-making jobs—which means that women are becoming both mentors and protégés in greater numbers than ever before.

The changes, though rapid, still have a way to go before they produce equality. Men still dominate most corporate power structures. Thus, if you are a woman, the statistical odds are that you will find more potential mentors of the opposite sex than of your own. Don't let this disturb you. A mixed-sex mentor relationship can be wonderfully productive. I've observed and admired several. A particularly appealing example was portrayed on TV a few years back in the *Mary Tyler Moore* show. Edward Asner played, to perfection, the role of a mentor of the Parent Figure type. In real life, such a mentor—tough but affectionate, fond of his power and fond of using it—can do much to strengthen his protégé's job security and steer good things her way.

The obvious danger, of course, is sex. If a man offers job favors in return for sexual favors, then he doesn't fit the definition of a true mentor and should be handled with the greatest caution, as should any false mentor. But sex problems can arise even in what starts out as a genuine mentor relationship. These problems are a special case of the general hazards of sex in the office. We'll study these hazards in detail later (Chapter 12). For now, let me sound these brief warnings:

Sex can be part of the glue that binds two people together, as in a marriage. But unless you are very careful and very lucky, it can enormously complicate your life if you allow it to become part of a mentor relationship. My advice: don't. Why take the risk? It may work out, but the odds are it won't. A sex-based relationship will expose you to whisperings, jealousies, and scandals, will cloud your judgment and your mentor's judgment of business situations and career problems. Avoid these complications if you can.

Be particularly careful about body language. Don't send out signals that you don't mean to send. Nonsexual touching and kissing come naturally to some people but not to all. Avoid them unless you are *absolutely* sure your mentor will interpret them in the way you intend—as gestures of simple liking. Better yet: avoid them entirely. Your mentor may interpret them correctly but some observer may not. Before you know it, you are the subject of gossip. The whispered rumor gets juicier as it goes from mouth to mouth. All that really happened was that you touched your mentor's hand to express your fondness—but the grapevine report is that you are involved in a torrid love affair.

You don't need that.

═Strategies ═══════════════════════════

The process of acquiring a mentor begins, of course, with identifying somebody who you think can fill this role for you. As we've seen, this might be your boss, somebody else with power in your department, or someone who isn't directly in line with your function but still is close enough to understand it well and to exert influence on your career. For example, let's say you work in a company's paralegal research department. Your mentor might be your boss, the chief of legal research; or perhaps the lawyer to whom your boss reports; or maybe another company lawyer who has no day-to-day contact with your work.

The person you pick must have power and the promise of more to come. Keep your ears open: whose name keeps coming up in conversations? Who is being talked about as potential top executive material?

The person you pick should also be someone with whom you think you can establish an amiable and mutually serving relationship. As we are going to see, the mentor relationship is a two-way street. You cannot merely take but must also give. Don't ask only, "Can this man or woman help my career?" Also ask, "What useful service can I offer?"

Don't be put off if your eye happens to alight on a potential mentor who already has a protégé. I've known mentors to have whole families of them. This sometimes happens when an executive moves through several companies, picks up a protégé at each, and stays in touch with them all and continues to follow and aid their careers after moving on. Or a mentor may adopt two or more protégés at the same place. It isn't common but isn't rare either. A mentor can have fond relationships with several protégés just as easily as a parent can love more than one child.

Don't rush this process of sizing up possible mentors. If you have been in your job or with the organization for a long time, you may already know where the power lies, whom to avoid, and so on. Indeed, perhaps you already have the beginnings of a relationship with a mentor but haven't actively pursued it—which, of course, I now urge you to do. But if you are new to the job, you must proceed more slowly.

Take time—six months if necessary, even a year—to understand the organization thoroughly. Who has the real power? Who is being readied for bigger things? Who is a protégé of the really powerful? (Yes: your mentor will in all likelihood be, in turn, the protégé of somebody still higher up. You may come in at the end of an entire chain of mentor-protégé relationships—and will yourself become a mentor, in time, to someone below you.)

As a newcomer you will probably be granted a honeymoon period—a time in which to learn the job, show what you can do, settle into the organization. Mistakes will be forgiven during this period; people will root for you and help you. That is pleasant—but be aware that this is also a period of high danger. People will be sizing you up, jockeying for position around you, assessing you as a possible future ally or enemy. For your safety, remember one rule and remember it well: during this period, *keep all your personal opinions to yourself.*

Stay strictly neutral. Don't take stands on matters you don't yet understand. Don't take sides. Don't get sucked into schemes. Politely rebuff all attempts to recruit you into alliances.

This is the period when people are going to buy you a drink or take you for a walk after lunch and ask, "Say, what do you think of Joe Smith?" *Don't answer*—or if you must say something, be neutral. Joe Smith could be your future mentor. The person quizzing you could be. You don't yet know enough about the place to start joining teams. Respond to the question by mumbling something polite: "Oh, he seems like a nice guy from what little I know of him."

Having identified one or several possible mentors, your next problem is to make yourself known to them and see whether a productive relationship can be established. How do you do this?

There are three kinds of action that I can recommend:

1. *Turn in a good job performance and make sure people know it.* Just as every parent wants bright kids who bring home good report cards from school, so a potential mentor is attracted to the best and the brightest. Remember that your mentor, in time, will be sticking his or her neck out for you, recommending you for promotions, writing praise-filled reports about you, making promises about your probable performance in this situation and that. You won't want to make a fool of your mentor by failing to live up to these expectations. Nor would your mentor enjoy such an outcome. Hence, he or she will be drawn, in the beginning, to somebody who shows promise of responding well to unknowable future challenges.

A woman executive at Union Carbide put it this way: "I don't have any special protégé. I'd like to. It would be rewarding. But this person would have to be somebody I could be proud of."

Turning in a superior job performance won't help you a great deal unless people know about it, of course. We'll study the techniques of personal publicity later (Chapter 7). Meanwhile, be aware of the need to catch the eye and ear of your potential mentor. If you put in extra hours at your job, doing more work than is actually required, find some casual and noncomplaining way to let this be known to many people. If someone praises you for the high quality of your work, look for a graceful way to broadcast this helpful fact.

2. *Ask your potential mentor's advice.* People enjoy being asked for advice; it flatters them, makes them feel important. Moreover, asking a possible mentor for advice is a way of instantly establishing the kind of teacher-student relationship you want. It gets you started on the right foot. But you must handle it intelligently.

Don't pester the man or woman with a lot of trivial questions. Rather find out what the person's major area of expertise is and ask just one or a few big questions: "I'm told your special field is cost accounting, Ms. Parker. I'm working on this Navy contract, and I've run into a problem that has me stumped . . ."

What you hope is that the mentor-to-be, flattered by your approach and intrigued by your problem, will take the time to give you a short course in certain aspects of cost accounting. "Sure, I'll be happy to help you. Why don't we get some coffee and go somewhere away from these phones . . ." That's the ideal outcome. If it doesn't happen—if the man or woman is busy, distracted, uninterested—don't try to wheedle more time than he or she is ready to give. Come back another day—or try another possible mentor.

And be sure you don't upset your boss by going outside the department for advice. Some bosses don't mind if their people roam around the company in search of needed answers; indeed, some encourage such roaming, on the theory that getting the job done right is what's important. Other bosses, however, resent any behavior that they interpret as sneaking around behind their backs or going over their heads.

We come back to what I said before about taking time to study your job environment with care before making moves to acquire a mentor. If you decide to approach a potential mentor at some remove from your daily work, be sure you know what your boss's reaction is going to be. Don't guess; *know.* If you are not sure, ask him or her. "This cost-accounting problem has me stonewalled. Somebody told me Ms. Parker is a genius at this kind of thing. Do you think maybe she could give me some guidance?"

3. *Offer to help with some specific problem.* First find out what is important to this man or woman, your potential mentor. What is worrying this person right now? It might be something temporary: a need to organize a sales meeting, for instance. Or it might be something quite trivial: perhaps the person has been sending out irritable memos about inefficient use of the company parking lot. Having discovered what is disturbing the man's or woman's sleep and digestion these days, do some research on it, some thinking, some looking around. Then go to the person and offer to lift some of those worries onto your own shoulders. "Mr. Willard, I heard you say you were concerned about getting those figures from the government in time for the meeting. Well, I made a few phone calls this afternoon, and it turns out there's a way . . ."

Concentrate on relatively small, even trivial problems. Don't make the mistake of marching into the person's office with a grandiose solution to a major problem: "I've worked out a way to increase the company's earnings next year!" Do that and you put yourself into a negative position. You are telling your potential mentor, in effect, that you see the big picture more clearly than he—more clearly than all the top executives who have been worrying about earnings for years. Perhaps you *do* see it more clearly, but it is a mistake to say so now. Wait a few years. In time, your thinking on the big questions may be sought, possibly by your mentor. You will then know you are heading for higher ground.

6

Leading a Task Group

Your first move into any kind of supervisory position—even if you have only two or three clerical workers under you— is a key test that could weigh heavily on your security and your future. It is a test whose results will be watched and analyzed by yourself and others. It will begin to answer questions that you can expect to face again and again in your business career:

Is this person capable of leading others?

Is he or she ready to take over a bigger and more powerful team?

Perhaps you have already passed that first test and are in the midst of a new one. The testing will never cease, not even if you become your company's president. All leaders—whether they head a three-person task group, a department, a division, or an entire company—must continually prove to themselves and to all those watching that they possess the ability to lead a group of people smoothly, efficiently, harmoniously, and contentedly toward a goal. Must prove, in other words, that they possess the quality we call leadership.

It often seems like an elusive and mysterious quality. There are some who find it so mysterious that they believe it can't even be defined. "It's something inside—who knows what it is?" says a Hemingway character. Others believe it is a quality you are born with or without. They think you can no more easily change your inborn leadership capacity than the color of your eyes.

I am perfectly sure none of this is true. The ability to lead a group well is, at its root, a simple and straightforward skill that can be learned by any intelligent man or woman. The finer points of this skill, like any skill, may take many years to master, but the fundamentals can be grasped and applied quickly.

The fundamentals are the same no matter where in the company hierarchy you may stand. You must learn them if you look forward to continued security and success in the business world. With few exceptions, any upward step in business means taking over leadership of a bigger or more important team. Whatever team you now lead, whatever team you hope or expect to be promoted into next, it is essential that you get those people together and form them into a group that works.

For if they perform their jobs poorly, it won't be their fault. In the eyes of management people above you, it will be yours.

Look, Listen, Ask

The crucial first step in getting a team together is to study it and its environment with the greatest care. Astonishing numbers of business group leaders fail to do this—including some top executives I've known.

This first, exploratory step—or, more accurately, series of steps—is something you should undertake as soon as you are assigned to lead any group. If you are already in a supervisory position but didn't conduct a careful exploration when you began the job, now is the time to do it. Better late than never.

These are the key parts of the exploration:

THE MISSION   Find out precisely what this group of people is supposed to accomplish. What is meant to be the end product of your group, and just how does it contribute to fulfillment of the company's all-encompassing goal?

Try to boil it down to a concise statement: "This company's goal is to make money for its stockholders by manufacturing and selling children's clothing profitably. My group is part of the accounts-receivable department, whose mission is to bill customers and monitor payments. The specific mission of my group is to get in touch with delinquent customers, find out what the problem is in each case, and take whatever action seems appropriate, always remembering that our main purpose is to get the money fast."

In seeking such a description of your group's goals, go to many sources, not just one. If there is a written function description in a manual or some other directive, start with that. If possible, talk to the person who headed your group before you; to executives above you who depend on what your group does; to people from other groups that interface with yours; and to your group members themselves.

You are likely to find that various people differ widely—even wildly—in their conceptions of what your group is supposed to do. This is why it is a bad idea to depend on just one source for your mission description.

Your group's previous leader, for example, may have been a man or woman who was afraid of taking responsibility for decisions, and who therefore went to considerable lengths to avoid making any decisions at all. This person's description of the group mission might well have a gaping hole in it:

"The mission? Yes, well, we're supposed to get in touch with delinquent accounts, find out what the problem is . . ."

Accurate so far, but the hole starts to appear:

". . . And then we route the case to whoever has authority to handle it. Like, if it's less than $100 we get the Billing people to send out a reminder. And if it's delinquent more than sixty days, we turn it over to Joe Williams in Collections. And if . . ."

In other words, your predecessor saw this group as nothing more than a traffic-switching operation. The whole purpose of the group, as your predecessor saw it, was to sort cases into categories and then unload them on other people—thus neatly evading all decision-making responsibility.

But if you talk to people above you, you may find that this is

precisely what they *don't* want. "Your group's main job is to handle
as many of these cases as you can by yourselves," a senior executive
may well tell you. "Use your heads. Use your imaginations. Do what
needs to be done. Don't pass the buck up here or over there unless
you really have to. We're all busy. We don't have time for a lot of
these cases. That's what *you* get paid for . . ."

THE JOBS   Your group will accomplish its mission, or will fall
short, in direct correlation with the members' performance in their
separate jobs. If they perform poorly, it could be mostly their fault—
but, as I remarked before, they won't get the bulk of the blame. You
will.

Your initial task, then, is to study their separate jobs—what they
are supposed to do, what they *think* they are supposed to do, and
what, in fact, gets done.

If there is any shortfall in the team's effectiveness in accom-
plishing its mission, you are likely to find the problem can be traced
to either or both of two roots:

1. Your people are blocked or hindered in some way in the
performance of their jobs. Or, more commonly . . .

2. Your people's perceptions of their jobs are off-target. The jobs
they are actually doing, in other words, are not the jobs that need
to be done in order to fulfill the group's mission.

The first kind of problem, a blockage or hindrance, is often
comparatively simple both to analyze and to fix. In one company
I'm familiar with, for example, there was a small team of people
whose function required them to spend a lot of time making and
receiving long-distance phone calls. The company's phone system
was antiquated. There were long waits to place outgoing calls; incoming calls often got misrouted and lost; connections were likely
to be broken at any time.

In this case it was the group leader's responsibility to be aware
of the problem, to understand how it reduced the group's effectiveness, and to do something about it. For years, the group had had a
leader who simply tried to shrug it off; the team's performance
seemed adequate to him, and he lacked the energy to try to improve
it. Then he was forced into early retirement, and a woman took

over. She made it her business to bring the group's problem to the attention of top management. She fought for her people. When a better phone system was finally installed, the group's productivity soared.

And she got the credit, of course. There are two sides to every coin. The leader gets most of the blame when a group fails—but gets the big prize when it succeeds. That woman has enjoyed steady raises and promotions ever since.

The second kind of problem—people's faulty perceptions of their jobs—is more common. It is particularly common among old-timers in a team—not necessarily older people, but those who have been on the team for a long time.

For one thing, you are likely to find veteran employees still operating under instructions they received years ago. In the interim many things may have changed: the company's markets, its procedures, its philosophy. But not all employees are aware of these changes or have figured out or been told how to adjust their job functions. This is why anachronisms are so common in the business world. You will see veteran employees laboriously entering figures in handwritten account books, though computerized records make all that work unnecessary.

For another thing, veteran employees tend to exaggerate the importance and sanctity of their own jobs. They become angry and defensive if you suggest that certain ritualized functions are unnecessary or can be pared down or done faster.

I recall being called in by a large company to evaluate a troubled department. Everyone in the department complained bitterly of being overworked, and casual observation did indeed produce an impression of frantic toil. People sat frowning over sheafs of paper, rushed from desk to desk, shouted into phones. Nobody could be accused of loafing. Yet the department was chronically late with its assigned tasks and at times failed to do them at all. What was wrong?

It turned out that the department consisted mainly of old-time people who, over the years, had gradually got themselves bogged down in details. They had lost sight of the department's fundamental goals and purposes. Instead, they had become concerned with trivia. Should such-and-such a report be typed on blue paper or pink?

Whose initials should appear on it, and in what order? At one time there may have been a sound reason for each of the minor procedural rules that entrapped these people, but in most cases the reasons were lost in the mists of time.

As an outsider coming fresh to the scene, I could see the problem plainly, but I knew it would not easily be made plain to the department's employees. People like to think of themselves and their jobs as important, and it is a mistake ever to make light of anyone's work, no matter how silly and trivial it may seem to you. If somebody has been laboriously sorting out blue and pink reports for years, you are surely going to meet resistance—and perhaps make an enemy— if you come around and say the work is valueless and ridiculous.

Instead of doing that, I approached the problem carefully—as you should do if and when you encounter it. Without in any way belittling what these loyal people had been doing, I managed to convey the idea that exciting new worlds were opening up for the company, and a lot of office procedures were to be streamlined to meet developing challenges. There was some grumbling, as there almost always is when any change is made in old routines, but nobody got seriously upset. In time, as the department's work speeded up and words of praise began to come down from the management levels above, the team's morale soared.

Just because most people *do* consider their jobs important, you always stand to make friends when you show a team how to get the mission accomplished better. People like the feeling of doing valued work and doing it well. As a team leader, you do neither yourself nor your subordinates a favor by simply relaxing, smiling at everybody, and letting the work plod along in well-worn ruts. Instead, study the group's mission, then talk to each of the members and find out whether the work actually being done directly serves that mission. If it doesn't, find out what work is blocked or hindered and what is off-target. Gently fix what needs to be fixed. You should feel the strengthening of the team almost immediately.

THE PEOPLE   While interviewing your subordinates about the way they perceive their jobs, you will also want to find out about them as people. Don't pry; just show interest.

In a previous chapter I counseled you to make overtures to a new boss. When the situation is reversed and *you* are the new boss, it will be up to you to make overtures to those of your subordinates who don't quickly show interest in getting to know you. Call each person into your office one by one if you have an office, or go to their desks if it seems more natural, or take them to the company cafeteria for a cup of coffee. Whatever you do, *don't* leave this initial acquaintance-making to chance. If you have been the leader of a team for some time and haven't yet had such orientation sessions with your people, do it as soon as you can.

You will want to find out, of course, how they perceive and perform their jobs. Also find out who the leaders of this peer group are. Every team, even the smallest, has an unwritten, unofficial organization—a pecking order. Sometimes it is the most senior employee who stands at the top of this order; sometimes it is the oldest; sometimes it is the smartest, sometimes just the loudest. Quite often it is a secretary who has been with the company for a good many years, knows all the gossip, knows or can guess who is marked for promotion and who for the discard pile.

Be sure to make friends with this unofficial leader. You may encounter hostility at first. He or she may have been fond of a group's previous boss, may have felt secure and coddled under the old leadership, may now feel worried, uncertain, and resentful. These are all perfectly natural reactions to an incoming new leader; don't let them upset you.

Instead, reassure the person that his or her position isn't in jeopardy from the change in bosses. A little subtle flattery may help: "You seem to have a thorough knowledge of what goes on around here. I'm going to rely on you to help me get myself oriented . . ."

Don't expect to be accepted instantly. Allow time for these people to watch you, and to speculate and gossip about you among themselves. Just be sure that they also do a lot of talking to you.

Getting Performance

When the initial exploration is over, you should have a basis for making the group into an efficient, performing unit. You now know three essential things:

1. What the mission is.
2. Where the drive toward that mission is being weakened by blockages or poor targeting.
3. What staff you have to work with.

Having gathered this information and sorted it in your mind until you clearly see how all the parts fit, you now begin to use it. Here is how to make the process work well:

□ Tell each subordinate just how *you* perceive the job he or she is to do. Be gentle but firm. Don't ridicule the work your people have been doing or laugh at their misperceptions, but do make it clearly understood that you want things done your way. Give reasons; show why you think your way is going to produce the best results.

□ Don't try to describe each person's job down to the last detail. Give these people credit for intelligence, give them the leeway to use it, and be sure they know you are giving it: "If you have problems with this, let me know, but I think it'll be better if I let *you* figure out the best routine . . ." You will have to use your human judgment about this. Some people need and want fairly close supervision, while others can take only a bare outline of a job and run with it.

□ Reward good performance *publicly and often*. Pay raises and promotions are the big plums of the business world, of course, but there is a limit to the number of such plums that can be handed out to a given employee, particularly in less-than-boom times. In any case, the supervisory jobs you hold early in your career might not give you much influence over salaries and promotions. But another kind of reward costs nothing and can be handed out often: the public commendation. "Before we get down to the business of the meeting, I want to say how good a job you're all doing. Martha, I thought you handled that problem beautifully last week . . ."

Martha will blush and pretend to be uncomfortable. But she will glow for the rest of the day. And she will try to perform even better tomorrow.

□ Admonish poor performance *privately* and in steps of increasing severity. Be very gentle the first time: "Sam, you left some blanks in this report. It's got to be filled out completely or Martha won't have enough information to work with. Is there some problem I can help with . . . ?" Let Sam do all the explaining he wants to do. In all likelihood, all you will hear will be the usual excuses people give for careless work: "I was rushed . . . I had to take care of such-and-such . . ." and so on. Don't argue or call Sam a liar. Just listen. It may be there actually *is* a problem you didn't know about, in which case, of course, you should do something about it. But if Sam merely mumbles excuses, be patient. With most people, one gentle admonishment is enough to produce more careful work.

If there is a second time, make the admonishment more severe: "Look, Sam, these incomplete reports cause a bottleneck we can't afford to have. This is the second time we've talked about this. You're slowing up Martha's operation, and that makes the whole group look bad."

The third time . . .

□ Firing is, of course, the ultimate punishment of the business world. Be very, very careful with it. Don't make frequent or idle threats about getting people fired. Save this ultimate remedy for the most extreme situations, when all else has failed. Even then, be sure you have firing authority before threatening or attempting to use it.

I recall talking to one fairly high-placed executive who had had a painful experience with a firing. During a period of companywide retrenchment, he fired a fifty-nine-year-old man who had failed to earn his salary for years. "The guy was lazy, insubordinate, and just plain incompetent at his job," the executive said. "I'd given him more chances than he deserved. Finally I let him go. A week later, he lands in a hospital with a heart attack. Oh boy! You wouldn't believe the problem it caused. I felt I had to stand by my decision; the guy was a malingerer and I didn't want him in my department, messing up my other people's work. But in the end, top management ordered me to take him back. They felt the overriding consideration was company morale."

Even the best-handled, most trouble-free firing is painful to both people involved. Avoid it as long as you can. On the other hand, never forget that the team's mission is of primary importance. If a subordinate continues to turn in a poor job performance and shows no interest in improving, and if you genuinely feel you have tried everything there is to try, then you had better talk to a senior executive and find out what kind of firing authority you may have.

□ Set standards, and publicize them both by directive and by example. Establish rules for promptness, for keeping schedules, for personal neatness. *And then exceed those standards yourself.*

If you want your people at their desks by nine each morning, you had better be at *yours* by 8:50. If you want them to improve the sloppy personal appearance tolerated by a previous boss, you had better pay meticulous attention to your own grooming. This doesn't mean you should dress more formally than is the custom in that particular level of the company. If everybody else is in casual wear, you might look out of place in a suit. But be sure *your* casual wear is spanking clean, well pressed, and neat.

7

Personal Publicity

J Paul Getty made his international name as an oil tycoon, but he was also an accomplished writer and a cogent career strategist. He wrote, among other things, thirty-four often sermon-like articles for *Playboy*, setting forth his views on how young career climbers should behave in their struggle for survival. Until his later years he was also happy to talk with reporters on this topic. He would answer questions gravely and thoughtfully, and sometimes would phone a reporter several days later to add some new ideas that had occurred to him on whatever they had talked about.

One of his favorite maxims consisted of four short words: *Be seen and heard.*

He recalled that he had once spent months scouring the world for a man or woman to fill a certain job in his oil empire. "The specifications were pretty demanding," he said. "The person had to be fluent in several languages, have a thorough command of inter-national finance, be able to read an engineering blueprint and have several other attributes, including personal charm. After looking for this rare bird for a long time, we finally found a fellow in Paris who more or less filled the bill. We hired him at a very nice salary. A year later I learned, by sheer chance, that we had a young chap in one of our American operations who would have fitted into the picture even better. Do you see what his mistake was? He didn't make himself known."

A bad mistake indeed. It is supremely frustrating when the world fails to recognize your accomplishments. Many people seem to feel the world owes them such recognition. They sit around hoping the applause and rewards will come to them automatically, and when nothing happens, they howl at the unfairness of it all.

They are right about one thing: the world is unfair. The career battleground knows nothing of fairness, and you should not expect any. If it happens, be grateful, but never build your hopes on it. To be sure that whatever you do is recognized, you must learn the art of personal publicity.

There are eight key components of this art:

═ *Taking On Challenges* ═══════════

One of the best ways to make a name for yourself in an organization is to take on tough, intimidating tasks that nobody else wants to touch. Take on risks. Yes, of course you may trip and fall. But as we've noted in another context, it isn't often that anybody's career is damaged by an isolated mistake. If you take on a tough task and fail at it, you dust yourself off and try something else.

Most successful people in business urge risk-taking as a personal policy. "Always be ready to take on challenges," counsels Martin R. Shugrue, who started his career as a pilot and is now Pan Am's senior vice-president of marketing. "Never mind about the risks. If you spend all your time worrying about risk, you probably aren't going to get anywhere."

Failure is part of life. Don't be afraid of it. For as President Harry Truman was fond of saying, "You can't win a game unless you're willing to lose it." Sooner or later there will come a time when you take on a challenge and win. That one bright victory can get you talked about more than years of steady, risk-free plodding.

Merely doing your job competently won't often win you much publicity, except in very small organizations. "Who's this Sheila

Smith on the overtime list?" Executive A will ask. Executive B replies, "Oh, I think she works in Quality Control someplace. Good worker, I've heard." Executive A nods, shrugs, and never thinks about Sheila Smith again.

The scenario can be much better. "Who's this Sheila Smith?" asks Executive A. Executive B says, "She's the one who went up to Chicago and straightened out that mess about the EPA records, remember?" Executive A says, "Oh, *she's* the one, is she? . . ."

The mess Sheila Smith straightened out may not have been very big or important. But by taking a risk, by being willing to fail, she has given people reason to remember her name.

Being Seen

Make a point of attending as many functions in and around the company as you reasonably can. Not all employees are invited to all functions, of course, but the average person does get invited to more than he or she really wants to attend. Never mind. Attend them anyway.

Go to meetings, seminars, after-hours groups, company picnics, free movies on health and safety, lectures by visiting economists. Many people assiduously stay away from all such voluntary gatherings, feeling that they have more interesting ways to spend their time. But you are not going to imprint your face on people's minds if you are seldom seen outside your office.

Job-Related Socializing

Also seize opportunities to spend unstructured time with people in the company and others who do business with it. If you go to a meeting and somebody suggests a cup of coffee afterward in the cafeteria, go and have that cup of coffee unless it really upsets your schedule. If it does, then make a point of suggesting an alternate time and be sure to follow through when the time comes. If somebody suggests a drink, go along; and if you don't want an alcoholic drink, sip ginger ale. If somebody suggests a breakfast meeting, accept enthusiastically even though you hate getting up early in the morning.

And initiate such socializing opportunities yourself. Whenever you feel comfortable with somebody, suggest lunch or a drink once in a while. It wouldn't be a good idea to try this with a boss you have just met, or with any superior with whom you have a distant and formal relationship. But if you and your boss or mentor arrive in time at a mutual easy, casual, friendly feeling, then it is perfectly acceptable and pleasant for you to broach the idea of an unstructured hour or so away from the office.

Don't approach this kind of job-related socializing in a cynical spirit. Some do—and, as a result, many people who are not in business careers seem to assume that all job-related socializing is joyless, manipulative, and money-oriented. This is certainly not true. There is no reason why people who work together cannot enjoy the simple pleasure of one another's company. The business world would be a cheerless place indeed if we all sat glumly in our offices and never spent a convivial hour together.

Moreover, work-related socializing makes the work go more smoothly and pleasantly. If you and some of your peers have lunch or a drink together once in a while, you all benefit from an improved understanding of each other both as task-group colleagues and as people. If you and your boss have a problem to discuss, you are likely to find that both of you think more creatively and interact more productively over a restaurant table than in an office setting.

And finally, this kind of socializing advances you toward your goal of becoming widely known. Today you spend some after-hours time with someone simply because you find him or her pleasant to be with. Tomorrow that person may be in a position to do you a career-making favor.

Talking About Your Job

You may feel you can do your job competently all by yourself; you need no help and would rather not have to put up with the interference. Even if you are convinced this is true, it is never a good idea to become isolated in a job. Instead of making yourself a hermit, you must go out of your way to talk to other people about what you are doing. You *and* your job should be as widely publicized as possible.

Ask others for advice, even if it's only to confirm a decision you've already reached on your own. It flatters people to be asked for advice. It is also a subtle way of saying, "Hey, look at me! Look at the complicated work I'm doing!"

Needless to say, you don't want to make a nuisance of yourself by phoning or going into somebody's office with mundane questions every day. Just once in a while, when you have the kind of question people can get their teeth into: "Mr. Prescott, I wonder if I could ask your advice. A peculiar problem has come up in our new billing system, and someone told me you once solved a similar . . ."

═ Memos ═

The memorandum or memo—business-world jargon for an office-to-office letter—can be an important publicity tool if you use it right. Most people don't.

The first rule of good memo-writing (or good letter-writing, for that matter) is to keep it brief. Anything longer than one single-spaced typewritten page is too long. Half a page is ideal.

The second rule is to prepare it in such a way that its gist can be gathered from a lightning-fast skim-reading. Many business executives riffle through their mail at high speed in the early morning or at night; they are practitioners of the skim-reading technique, in which the eye sweeps down the page and slows only when it encounters key sentences and phrases. So make it easy for your readers; make sure your point isn't buried. To help it stand out, use typographical tricks such as underlining. This draws attention to main points and gives readers a quick understanding of the way you want them to organize various thoughts in their minds. The paragraphs you are now reading are written and displayed in this way.

The third rule: use pleasant, friendly, informal language, fa-

voring short words and short sentences. Studiously avoid two ex-
tremes: don't let your language sound stiff or pompous, but on the
other hand don't let it degenerate into the cute or slangy. Pompous
language is irritating, causes some to dislike the writer, and leads
others to dismiss him or her as a show-off; while cute or slangy
language makes many uncomfortable and may actually offend some.
Write simply and directly, as you normally talk.

The fourth rule: don't allow your memos to sound arrogant or
give off an air of a know-it-all. A memo in which you are directly
issuing orders to subordinates can of course have the sound of
confident authority, though even that should never sound pompous.
But any memo circulating to peers or superiors must contain at least
a hint of humility. Avoid the sound of someone issuing final judgments: "I have decided that the way to solve this problem is . . . We
intend to issue instructions to the effect that . . ." Instead, make it
sound as though you seek advice, will welcome comment, have been
and will continue to be a good listener: "After many talks with the
individuals involved, my present feeling is that the way to solve this
problem may be . . . However, the question is complex. I'll welcome
any insights or suggestions . . ."

═Bragging Without Bragging═

Be careful to publicize any achievement you consider important—passing an educational milestone, for instance, or finishing
some challenging task. To do this, you must learn the technique of
bragging without bragging.

Undisguised, direct bragging annoys people: "I finally solved
that billing problem, and Mr. Prescott said he thought I handled it
brilliantly . . ." You win few friends that way. Some will be jealous.
Some will wonder why they should have *their* work interrupted so
you can crow about *your* triumph. Some will be bored. All will wish
you would go away and shut up.

So seek ways to spread the news without directly bragging. You
can mention your triumph obliquely in a memo, for example: "After
seeing our problem of the missing bills resolved, I've been asked to

tackle something else on which I'll need your help . . ." Or you can use a technique that we looked at in another context—asking for advice: "Ms. Baldwin, maybe you can give me some guidance. I've just finished a night course in computer programming, and I'm trying to figure out what direction to go in from here . . ."

Still another good way to publicize an accomplishment, if you handle it carefully and don't try it too often, is to organize an informal celebration in your own honor. Just be sure you don't bill it as a celebration of your own great brainpower. Instead, it is a celebration of the end of an arduous uphill climb. "I finally finished that computer course," you tell your colleagues. "What a relief! From now on my evenings are my own, and I'm going to use this first one for some fun with people I like. How about joining me for a drink after work . . . ?"

═In-Company Media ═══════

Many companies, divisions, and even smaller departmental units maintain publications that carry news and features about their people. These publications range in size and elegance from glossy magazines to single-sheet newsletters. It is worth noting that companies tend to keep them going even during times of desperate cost-cutting. Why? Because they are not considered a frivolous expense. In the words of a former editor of Union Carbide's *HQ News:* "These in-house publications get read. You'd be surprised how well they get read. By top management, among other people."

The moral is obvious: seize opportunities to get your name and accomplishments written up in any media published around your place of work.

You may be pleasantly surprised to find how easy it is to do this. Oddly, the competition for space in the average house organ isn't keen. Quite the opposite, in fact. "We often had to beg people to give us news," the Union Carbide ex-editor says. "It's like pulling teeth."

Most people in the business world are either too modest or too busy or too lazy to spend the small amount of time necessary to get their stories properly told in workplace media. Don't make any such mistake. Speak to your house-organ editor or newsletter writer. The chances are you will find him or her starved for good stories and eager to hear yours.

It goes without saying that you must have a story to tell. Wait until you are doing some interesting work and have saved up a few anecdotes and some cogent thoughts about it. Or wait until you have achieved something special: a promotion, an educational diploma. Then seek out the editor and tell the story in a bright, anecdotal way.

═ *Outside Media* ═

Publicity in media not associated with your company is valuable in less direct ways. Much of this outside publicity will filter back into the company; your boss and others will read about you and think what an interesting person you are. (You should make sure this happens, of course, by bragging without bragging anytime you make it into an outside publication.) Another value of outside media is that executive recruiters read them. As we will see in a forthcoming chapter, it is excellent strategy to get yourself noticed by recruiters even though you have no plans to relinquish your job.

The outside media most open to news and features about business people are:

□ *Journals of professional societies.* If such a society exists in your field, join if you can—and then send in news about yourself (or get your company public-relations department to do so) when you pass important milestones or have some other interesting story to tell.

□ *College alumni publications.* Most are hungry for news of alumni and alumnae.

□ *Newspapers, particularly local ones.* Large metropolitan dailies publish news of job promotions and other executive changes, but generally limit themselves to top-management goings-on. If you aren't in top management, you are likely to find a welcome in smaller newspapers published in your home town or county.

□ *Trade journals.* Unless you are in top management, it isn't likely you will see your name and picture in *Fortune* or any other general business magazine, but smaller magazines devoted to specific industries, trades, or professions are often happy to get news from readers. Many such magazines operate on tiny budgets and cannot afford large staffs of reporters. They depend on people such as you to supply them with news and features.

These are the four types of publications in which your outside publicity campaign is most likely to bear fruit. More rarely, you may get other opportunities. A local TV or radio station may want to interview you about local economic conditions, for instance. Or your company's board chairman may retire, and a newspaper reporter may phone you and ask for comment.

Be sure to consult with your boss and the public-relations department, if there is one, on all your outside publicity activities. This is a matter of common courtesy and is also for your own protection. Remember, you can get into trouble with your boss and others by appearing to do things secretively. The PR director may be jealous of his or her bailiwick and could become highly annoyed if you get yourself into a lot of outside media without consultation. So talk to the PR people; tell them what you're up to. If nothing else, it will make them happy—and perhaps they can give you some solid help.

Unless your company has rigid rules on the subject, you don't normally need to clear everything with the PR chief before releasing it to the press. Suppose you are commenting on the retiring chairman, and you say something innocuous: "He did a lot for this company, and we're sorry to see him go." It is hard to imagine how a statement like that could make anybody mad. So you are probably safe in releasing it to the inquiring reporter—just so long as, shortly afterward, you pick up your phone and tell the PR people what you have done.

But suppose the reporter is probing for a hot story. He says, "I have it from a reliable source that your board chairman was involved in a kickback scandal a while back. What do you know about that?" In this case, only one answer is possible for you: "I can't comment until I clear it with the PR people."

The reporter will be annoyed and angry. He will grumble to his editor about getting the "usual corporate runaround." Never mind. Don't feel sorry for the reporter. It's *your* job that is at stake.

8

How to Get Yourself Transferred

C. Hazard, a stockbroker and author of *Confessions of a Wall Street Insider* (Playboy Press, 1974), has watched many promising men and women come and go in his turbulent business. "One fact stands out for me," he says. "It's this: people make the same mistakes in their careers that they make as investors."

One of the most common mistakes, he says, is quitting too quickly. "So many times a new investor will come into the stock market, play around for a while, lose some money, get disgusted, and back out. I try to argue with this man or woman. 'Stick around,' I'll say. 'Take the trouble to learn what you're doing. You'll get better.' But no, the guy hasn't made an overnight killing, so right away he wants to quit."

People behave the same way in their careers, says Hazard, who started as a brokerage trainee many years ago and eventually rose into top management. "Time and again I see people come into a good promising job, but it doesn't go a hundred percent right for them, so right away they want to quit," he says. "I don't know how many times I've had people in my office, trying to get them to stay

93

and work things out. Good people, a lot of them, people who had a real future in this business. 'Stick around,' I tell them. But no, they've had a dispute with their boss, or they aren't getting a promotion they thought somebody promised them, so the answer is: quit. It's too bad."

Hazard says he recently met a women who had worked under him many years ago. She had joined his brokerage house as a secretary but had expressed interest in moving up to the position of customer's representative, or "rep." Since she was bright and personable, with an unusually keen understanding of the financial markets, the brokerage house was happy to accommodate her. "We went out of our way to help her get the schooling she needed," Hazard recalls. Her future was bright. But then, through a misunderstanding, she got blamed for a costly error that she did not believe was her fault. The problem could have been worked out, given patience on all sides, but she quit in anger.

That was in 1974, a notoriously bad year in and around Wall Street. She was never able to find a similar opportunity. By quitting, she had given her future away. She is still doing clerical work.

Quitting often seems like the easy way out of a bad situation. There is always a temptation to give vent to the emotions of a painful moment, to lash out, to act in anger. "When people quit," Hazard says, "they often do it partly in a spirit of revenge. They think, 'I'll show that so-and-so!' They think they're punishing those they leave behind, when they're really punishing themselves."

Hazard is right. Instead of quitting your job, you are usually better off sticking around and trying to improve what you've got. It takes more discipline to do that, of course, but it usually pays off.

Even if you feel your situation is intolerable, quitting may not be the best answer. I suggest a better one: get yourself transferred to another job in the same company.

The Reasons for Moving

A campaign to get yourself transferred will take a lot of planning and a lot of work. (As I said, quitting is easier.) So don't undertake such a campaign for trivial reasons: you find your boss too sharp-tongued; you are a bit disappointed with your last promotion. The reasons behind such a move should be solid and compelling.

There are six such reasons:

□ *You find yourself in a state of permanent boredom.* You get no stimulation from your work, hate to come to the office in the morning, can't wait to get out at night.

Everybody has occasional boring days or weeks. Everybody gets assigned to boring tasks once in a while. Obviously you wouldn't want to take drastic action if your feeling of stagnation has lasted only a short time or if you can see its end not far off. But when boredom becomes a permanent aspect of life, then it is a danger signal. It means the time may have come for a change.

□ *There are objective signs that your career is at a standstill.* These signs, coupled with the subjective sense of boredom or stagnation, may reinforce your suspicion that you are in a dead end.

The most important objective signs of career advancement are raises, promotions, and increased responsibility. Compare yourself with others of your own general age, educational background, and job level. Do most of them seem to be generating appreciably more forward motion than you? If so, then you may find it worthwhile to think of getting yourself moved.

□ *You find yourself trapped in an intolerable and unfixable personality or business-philosophy clash with your boss.* Not just an argument, not just a week-long period of anger, but a deep-rooted incompatibility that, in your best judgment, is permanent. You've tried hard and earnestly to fix it and now genuinely feel you have exhausted all feasible approaches. Looking ahead, you see virtually no hope that the situation is going to change in the near future.

□ *Having made a close study of your department or group, as I counseled in a previous chapter, you find it too far from lines of power and unlikely to get any closer in the foreseeable future.* The indications are that you are in a Siberia, where, if you don't do something to help yourself, you will freeze.

□ *Studying your boss in the same way, you find him or her to be a person of little or no real power.* In your best judgment, this situation is probably not going to change.

It is entirely conceivable that you could judge yourself to be in a weak department or group, but one with a strong, active, and ambitious boss who shows promise of lifting the team out of the mud in which it has been stuck. In that case, you would be well advised to stay put at least for a while and see what happens. But if you find a combination of weak department *and* weak boss, then you can profitably begin to think about getting yourself moved out.

□ *You feel, paradoxically, that you are a victim of your own success.* You have done such outstanding work, which has reflected such credit and glory on your boss, that he or she is now reluctant to let you go. Promotions you'd hoped for have not materialized. You have the distinct feeling that your boss intends to hold on to you until long past the time when, under normal circumstances, you would be moved up to the next level of rank and responsibility.

These are the six ruling reasons for seeking a transfer. Any one of them, if solidly based on tangible facts, is reason enough for making such a move.

Right Ways and Wrong Ways

If you determine that a move is warranted in your case, take warning: you are about to embark on a highly hazardous course. Handle it right and you can vastly improve both your present and your future. Handle it wrong and you can seriously damage your career. You can even wreck it.

So be careful. Here are the most important do's and don'ts:

Do let your dissatisfaction be known—very carefully and pleasantly, however, taking note of all the cautions below.

Don't just stew silently. Many people do that. I know one woman who boiled internally for years, never telling anyone she felt mired and frustrated where she was. Then, suddenly, she boiled over one day in her boss's office, shouted criticisms that she later wished she could take back, and ended up getting herself fired. Her boss was bewildered. "If only she'd *told* me how unhappy she was," he complained to me, "I'd have been glad to help her. Matter of fact, a couple of times in the past year I'd heard of job openings where I thought she'd fit neatly, but I didn't say anything. I thought she was perfectly content where she was!"

Do talk first to your immediate superior, your boss. Be pleasant and positive: "I've appreciated the chance to learn under you. You've been a great teacher. I kind of feel I'm ready for a new challenge now. Do you happen to know of anything opening up . . . ?" It's true that not all bosses will be softened or will react generously to this kind of approach, but I venture to say the majority will. Few, at any rate, will be angered by it. When someone comes up to you asking for important help, it isn't easy to say no.

Don't under any circumstances, allow your boss to hear of your get-transferred campaign from somebody else. I've known many people who tried to hide such campaigns from their superiors, and I can assure you that the chances are such an attempt will end badly—perhaps disastrously. Put yourself in your boss's position: wouldn't you be angry if you found out that a member of your team was sneaking around looking for another team to join? Of course you would—especially if you had made some kind of emotional investment in this straying team member. So be particularly careful about this: your boss should be the first, not the last, to know of your feelings, plans, and moves. You might as well tell your boss all about it in any case, for your chances of keeping such a campaign hidden permanently are just about zero.

Do talk to your mentor, if you have one—or, if you don't, to any company executives you think might help. Maintain your positive attitude: "I like this company and I want to stay, but I seem to have reached a point where I'm not making a great deal of progress. Can you suggest anything . . . ?"

Don't make this campaign into an assault on your boss. Never complain or whine: "I just can't get along with that woman. She makes mistakes and I end up getting blamed for them. She doesn't really have the qualifications . . . ." That kind of talk only makes people uncomfortable. Moreover, it can backfire, for the person you complain to may be a friend and admirer of your boss. No matter how badly your relationship with your boss has deteriorated, grin and bear it for the time being. Keep up your positive attitude and speak only kind words.

Do build roads in all directions while waiting for something good to appear. Seize opportunities to do unfamiliar kinds of work, learn new skills, meet new people. If you can identify a kind of work you'd like to do in a department that seems to be well plugged in to a line of power, then set up a course of schooling for yourself; become proficient in that work so that you will be ready to move into job openings as they appear. The schooling can be formal: a college extension course, perhaps, or a special education program offered by the company itself. Or the schooling can be entirely informal; it might involve nothing more than studying some books in a library. The point is to prepare yourself for whatever opens up.

Don't be impatient. It may take many months for things to fall into place. Don't issue ultimatums: "If I don't get transferred out of this department by the end of the month, I'm leaving!" You may be leaving.

Do see to it that the personnel department, if there is one, stays properly updated on changes in your schooling experience, and ambitions. Many personnel departments (sadly, not all) try to match new job openings with the skills and wishes of people already on the payroll; these people get early shots at new jobs before outsiders are invited to apply. Thus, if you are in the public-relations department but burn to get into test marketing, be sure to let the personnel people know about the courses you've been taking and the weekend consumer-interviewing work you've been doing. Also update your mentor at the same time.

Even If You're Happy

These do's and don'ts are specifically designed for the employed person who is actively dissatisfied with present and future prospects. But I believe you can profit from the advice even if you are entirely content in your present situation.

The advice is something like fire insurance. You hope you will never have to use it, but . . .

You never know what lies ahead. Today you seem to be solidly installed in a strong department under a powerful and generous boss who thinks the world of you. What can go wrong?

Any number of things.

You simply never know. Your boss could get promoted away from you, recruited out of the company, cut down in a power struggle, or fired. You could stumble in your own career, could make some expensive mistake, could be blamed for someone else's mistake. The nature of the company might change; a large company could acquire it and reorganize it; currently strong departments could be weakened or even abandoned completely. Your very profession—your particular area of expertise—could diminish in importance as the world's technological and social revolutions roll on.

So it never does any harm to be prepared for a change. Some people never see themselves as doing anything different; they blandly assume they will work contentedly and profitably in the same specialized area throughout their lives. These people are in grave danger. Don't get caught in this trap. Build roads for yourself, just in case you need them. Prepare escape routes. Study your current specialty, yes; become superior in it if you can—but don't close your eyes to all other possibilities.

Janet R., a General Motors employee, is one woman who knows from firsthand experience that this policy can pay off. She joined the huge company years ago, rising to a minor supervisory position in a divisional advertising office. "I always thought I was perfectly secure," she says. "I mean, GM! The biggest manufacturing company on earth! How could anything ever hurt GM? Just the same, in the late 1970s I started to ask myself if I wanted to be in advertising all my life. I looked around to see what else was going on, and for some reason I got interested in the way the annual report was put together. It was just a short step from there to the whole field of stockholder relations. I got more and more interested. I thought that would be a fine field to work in if I ever wanted a change."

Still without any suspicion that her advertising job would one day be in jeopardy, Janet R. started asking questions casually around the company. Who designed the annual report? Who decided what to tell the stockholders? She talked to her mentor, who happened to be her boss. This man had had some peripheral contact with the annual-report preparation process years before, when he had worked at Detroit headquarters. Amused by her interest, he introduced her by phone one day to a woman in Investor Relations. The woman invited Janet to visit if she was ever in Detroit.

Janet eventually took the woman up on this invitation. The woman introduced her to others in various functions bearing on the giant company's continual efforts to keep its far-flung stockholders informed and content. One older executive was particularly impressed by Janet's interest. He gave her some books to read. She read them and was very careful to return them with thanks a few weeks later.

"I didn't know it at the time," Janet says, "but I was working out my own salvation. This industry collapsed in the early eighties, as everybody knows. It wasn't just a recession for us, it was a full-scale depression. A lot of plants and offices either cut back on operations or closed down completely. In my office everybody was scared. We could see the writing on the wall. Some of the clerical staff were the first to be let go. Then the axe started to fall on people of my level. I knew I had to act fast, so I did. I called the man who had loaned me those books."

He was glad to hear from her. GM's management had some difficult explaining to do to stockholders—as did the managements of many other troubled companies. Stockholders were going to have to live with painful cuts in earnings, dividends, and, inevitably, the stock's market price. The company's posture toward its stockholders and the general investment community was undergoing radical change, and in the process job openings were being created. Janet was transferred out of her advertising job in the nick of time.

"I was lucky," she likes to say. But perhaps that is not quite accurate. I prefer to say she was prepared.

9

Using Time Well

Not long ago I telephoned the chief executive officer of a Fortune 100 Company. His secretary told me he was busy but would call me back. An hour later, he did.

That says much about this man's ability to use his time well. You might suppose that the highest-placed executives would be the most frantically busy and therefore the least likely to return phone calls promptly. But it is not so. With few exceptions, the opposite is true. High-placed people like this man are the ones who return calls quickly and courteously. The people who make you wait for days—or, worse yet, don't even trouble to return calls at all—are almost always in middle management or below.

And, unless they learn to do better, will probably stay there.

How does a CEO of a very large and complicated company manage to return a phone call in an hour? Is it that he is less busy than others, has less on his mind, less to do? Not likely. The answer is that he knows how to get the most out of his minutes and hours. This skill has undoubtedly been among the factors that have helped him climb so high.

The higher you go in the business world, the more complex

your life will become, the more problems you will be required to take care of, seemingly all at once, and the more desperately you will need the ability to utilize time. Without this ability you will be severely handicapped. Others who do have it will leap ahead of you. At best, lack of the skill will hold you back; at worst, the lack can wreck your career.

I recall a very sad case. It involved the sales director of a small auto-parts manufacturing company and its ad agency.

In the course of a business trip, one of the ad agency's account executives stumbled onto a lively lead. A large company had a sudden need for certain parts made by the smaller outfit. It needed them in very big quantities, and it needed them in a hurry.

Any ad agency likes to do what it can to boost clients' sales. The higher the sales volume goes, the better the ad experts look. The account executive therefore placed a phone call to his client's sales director, intending to pass on the lead for fast action. The sales chief's secretary said he was in a meeting, but she would have him call back.

Unfortunately for him and his company, he didn't.

The problem was that he had a habit of putting off tasks that he considered unpleasant. He thought he knew what the ad agency man was calling about: the agency contract was in process of renewal, and there had been a lot of argument over certain clauses. The sales director had not reached any final decisions about these clauses and didn't want to face the ad people's impatience. He knew he would have to do so sooner or later, but he was a chronic procrastinator. And so he failed to return the account executive's call.

After waiting a day, the account executive called again. He asked the sales director's secretary to tell her boss the call was urgent.

She reported this promptly to the sales director. This time he decided he would return the call at his earliest opportunity. However, he was now in the midst of one of the frenzies that overcame him from time to time. He had put off many other chores besides that one phone call, and now—as will inevitably happen—several of them had abruptly grown to crisis proportions. Panic reigned in his office. Another day went by before he was finally able to pick up the phone and return the account executive's call.

He was too late. The potential big customer had taken its business elsewhere.

That large order, and the repeat business that could have followed, would have done wonders for the smaller company's earnings statement. Nobody played tattletale against the sales chief, but the story was bound to drift around. Eventually, by chance, the president heard it. The sales director had been in trouble over procrastination before. This was the last straw. He was fired.

═ *The Key* ═══════════════════════════

This chapter is not about timesaving techniques in an efficiency expert's sense. There are countless numbers of such techniques and tricks: making lists and schedules, overlapping and combining similar tasks, and so on. These must be tailored to individual personalities and specific jobs. What works for me in my daily activities might have no relevance to you or your job.

But I can give you the main key to good use of time—the one element without which nothing else will work. It is this:

Don't put off what you don't want to do.

That is the big secret of time use, the secret known to successful executives. Put nothing off. If something must be done, do it promptly. Never procrastinate over tasks that irritate you, scare you, upset you, or displease you for any reason. If you know you've got to do them sooner of later, *do them now.*

Failure to obey this cardinal rule is the most important single reason why business people get into situations of intolerable time pressure. If you keep shoving unpleasant or annoying tasks into your bottom desk drawer, it is virtually certain that, at some future time, two or more of them will rise up simultaneously and demand instant attention. Note my choice of words. I didn't say it is possible or probable; I said it is *virtually certain.* You can count on it. The more tasks you push into that bottom drawer, the more fearsome and intractable is the time panic you are preparing for yourself.

What happens to people who put off tasks is that they get

trapped in a crisis situation. Events start happening to them so fast that they can only react instead of anticipating. They can barely resolve one problem before a new one appears. As the frenzy quickens, more and more tasks get put off. The tasks lie about, ferment, and eventually develop into problems requiring panicky action.

The supply of back-to-back crises becomes continuous. The unfortunate procrastinator is now chronically pressed for time. This is the kind of person who will not return your phone calls for days, if ever.

═ *The Roots of Procrastination* ═

There are four main reasons why business people put off tasks and get themselves into fearful time binds. The four are mortal enemies of yours. I urge that you get to know them, recognize them on sight, and be prepared to strike them down as soon as they appear. They are:

SINGLE-PROJECT ORIENTATION   This situation arises when you let one project assume overwhelming importance in your life. A project may rise to exaggerated status because it has some special personal interest for you, or because your boss has overemphasized its importance to him or her, or because you see it in some way as a project that can make or break your career. Whatever the wellspring may be, the result is that you devote inordinate amounts of time to this one special project, and you put everything else aside.

You can be perfectly sure of one thing. Sooner or later, the "everything else" will confront you.

Except in situations of extreme crisis, try never to let any one project overwhelm all else. Certainly, there will be times when one project will assume special importance and will require more personal input than other tasks. But be sure those other tasks get done all the same—done on time and done well.

FEAR OF AN UNPLEASANT CONFRONTATION   This was the particular problem that caused the downfall of the sales director I mentioned earlier. He put off returning the ad executive's phone call because he expected some mild unpleasantness. He thought the ad man was going to demand faster action on some delayed decisions. As it turned out, he was wrong; the ad executive was really calling about something else. But that is beside the point. The point is that putting off tasks is almost bound to get you in trouble one way or another, sooner or later.

Mildly unpleasant confrontations are a fact of daily life in the business world. There is simply no escaping them. We all realize that. We also realize how silly it is to try to duck such confrontations, for with rare exceptions, they aren't all that painful. All the same, it is an almost universal human tendency to put them off.

You've promised an associate some figures, but for some reason they are not ready. He is waiting to hear from you. You know you should call and explain the reasons for the delay, but you don't want to handle his annoyance. So you put the call off.

You need to discuss a project with your boss, but you expect her to be grouchy because the project isn't going well. So you keep walking past her office door instead of going in.

Familiar? Of course. Just about everybody is tempted to put off confrontations that threaten to be less than pleasant. But the most successful people in business learn not to give in to the temptation. They are too keenly aware that procrastination almost always leads to time panic.

Even if that were not so, it would still be a good idea to get confrontations over with promptly. They are usually so painless that afterward you wonder what you were worried about. Moreover, people appreciate it when you communicate with them on some project or problem they've been waiting to hear about—even if all you communicate is bad news.

People can handle bad news. What they dislike most of all is sitting and waiting for a phone call that never comes.

So don't make people wait. Pick up your phone and say it straightforwardly: "I'm sorry, but we haven't found that missing file yet. We're working on it. I just thought you'd want to know we haven't forgotten you."

Your hearer *will* appreciate knowing that. Furthermore, by making this quick call you have advertised some good things about yourself. You have communicated the fact that you care. And even though you have been obliged to report a lack of success in finding a missing file, you have still managed to convey a sense of your own efficiency. You are on top of the problem. You haven't swept it into a dark corner, forgotten it, or buried it under a pile of other problems.

Score one for you. You have extracted some good out of what might have become a bad situation.

If there is a good reason why you cannot make such a call yourself, have a colleague or subordinate do it: "George got called out of town unexpectedly, but he knows you're concerned about that file, so he asked me to give you a call . . ." This, too, shows care and consideration and gives an impression of efficiency.

FEAR OF DIFFICULTY   We also put off tasks that promise to be tough or onerous. I don't know how many times I have seen men and women stumble into this pitfall.

I remember one woman who managed a cost-accounting department. The company controller became concerned about a certain operation that wasn't working properly, and he asked her to review it and strengthen it. The assignment looked complex and difficult; among other complications, it was going to require finding people and putting together a temporary task team. So the woman put the project off.

The controller assumed it was being done.

Inevitably, a crisis came to a head. Such a crisis could have been predicted by the famous "Murphy's Law," which states that if something can go wrong, it will—and at the worst possible time. The crisis involved the troubled operation in the cost-accounting department. The company president wanted to know why this operation had been allowed to deteriorate so badly. He barked at the controller, who in turn barked at the cost-accounting manager. When she sheepishly admitted that she hadn't even begun to work on the troubled operation, she was relieved of her duties.

Somebody else took over the assignment. It turned out to be much easier than the woman executive had feared. The new cost-accounting chief not only straightened out the troubled operation but, in the process, inadvertently stumbled onto an idea for gaining substantial new cost savings. He emerged as a hero. Today he is the company's controller.

My advice: do the seemingly hardest tasks first. Many or most will turn out to be easier than you expected, thus relieving you of a burden of worry and clearing the rest of your day or week for the easier, more pleasant tasks.

Don't push projects and chores aside and allow them to turn into time bombs. Every task properly and promptly completed is a crisis that won't happen.

IRRITATION   Finally, we put off chores simply because they are irritating.

Trivial examples of this happen every day in both business and personal life. I know a man, for instance, who dislikes paying bills. It isn't that he finds the chore difficult; nor is it financially painful, for he has plenty of money. The problem is simply that he finds the task irritating.

And so, every month, he puts it off. Inevitably, this triggers a series of crises. Creditors begin dunning him. Credit-card companies, department stores, and others rebill him with added finance charges and late-pay penalties, which he hates to pay, thus creating still bigger problems. Finally, several times a year he has to spend almost an entire weekend in a time panic while he lays all the growing crises to rest.

His total expenditure of time per year is probably twice or three times as great as if he took care of the irritating chore promptly each month. He undoubtedly knows this. Yet he still cannot stay ahead of the game.

I don't know anything about this particular man's business life. But I would venture to guess he is the kind of man who experiences frequent, if not chronic, time panics. I would also give you odds that he doesn't return phone calls promptly.

This isn't a book of medical advice, but it should be mentioned that a life full of time pressure is notoriously the kind of life doctors warn against. Time pressure leads to jangled nerves, upset stomachs, headaches. The time-panicked person may also suffer in terms of personal relationships. This is the kind of person who barks at spouse and kids, talks brusquely or even rudely to subordinates and office colleagues, alienates friends.

Life goes much more smoothly if you get the irritating tasks— as well as the painful and seemingly difficult ones—out of the way quickly. Make promises to yourself: all phone calls are to be returned on the day received, all mail is to be answered within one day, and so on. And then hold yourself to those promises.

I've seen executives go to seemingly ridiculous lengths to keep themselves from piling up pushed-aside chores. One woman keeps a large accordion file on a side table in her office. The file is labeled, in large red letters, "PENDING." She explains: "That used to be where I put all my unanswered mail, memos about things to be attended to, unpaid bills, reports I was supposed to read, and so on. It used to bulge with paper. A time came when I got into such a crisis over things I hadn't done that I almost lost my job. That taught me a lesson."

She keeps the file in sight to remind her of the danger it represents. It is nearly always empty.

10

Protecting Your Flank

I n the business world there are many who will resort to almost any scheme to gain a career advantage, fair or not. Somehow you must develop strategies against these people without yourself becoming another ruthless schemer.

I've talked a lot about career strategy in this book. I want to pause briefly now to be sure you understand the difference between the kind of strategy I advocate and Machiavellian scheming.

The strategy I advocate is entirely positive. Its aim is to strengthen your hold on your job, not to undercut others or damage their careers. It seeks to give you career advantages, but only fair ones. Moreover, it doesn't stop with your own personal concerns but encompasses many other people's concerns as well. I've urged you to be supportive of your boss, for example, and to take actions that will benefit your company.

In contrast to this, the schemer's strategy is negative and selfish. It seeks to gain advantages by hurting others. Its scope is narrow: it is designed to benefit one person without regard to broader consequences that may affect others or even damage an entire company.

I know a woman who schemed in this way. She held a minor executive position in a bank. Eager for more salary and status, she set out deliberately to make friends at higher management levels. This in itself was fine; indeed, I've advised you to do just that in seeking a mentor and for other reasons. She did it negatively and selfishly, however.

Instead of supporting the boss of her department, she spread tales of his incompetence. It was true the department was functioning poorly, but mismanagement by the boss was not the only reason. The woman herself was causing some of the problems by failing to pay close enough attention to her assigned duties. She devoted most of her time to self-serving strategies instead of trying to help the group get itself together. She also undercut many of her peers in the department. She tried to make it seem as if most of the good work turned out by the department was her doing.

The scheming worked for a time, as often happens. She impressed management and was eventually made the boss of her department. However, the department's performance immediately went from bad to worse. The new boss's subordinates, her former peers, rebelled. Many asked for transfers. When it became apparent to management that the new boss was incapable of holding the team together, she was moved to another part of the company. Her dreams of a management career faded away.

Scheming of that kind rarely pays off in the long run. However, it can produce short-term advantages—and those could be at your expense if you are the one being schemed against. You must be prepared to protect yourself against unfair assaults from three directions: from subordinates, from superiors, and from peers.

═ Defenses Against a Subordinate ═

In a large international company, a young lawyer subtly spread the rumor that his boss, also a lawyer, was a secret drinker. He coveted her job and had long sought some method of getting her out of the way. In truth, she drank only lightly on social occasions and never during a working day. However, she had a middle-ear ailment that sometimes affected her balance. She was sometimes seen bumping into doorframes, and occasionally she had to lean on something for a second after standing up from a chair. When the young man called attention to these lapses, executives began to watch her and wonder about her—just as he intended.

In another situation, a man was denied a promotion that he felt he deserved. The reason for the denial was incompetence, but he took it as a personal attack against him by his boss, and he schemed to get even. He saw his chance when he and his boss attended an important sales meeting in a distant city. The boss was to give a key talk at this meeting. The vengeful subordinate secretly saw to it that when the boss stood up to speak he had all the wrong papers with him and made a fool of himself.

A subordinate may scheme against you for career advantage or for some less pragmatic reason, such as spite. It may be very subtle, so much so that for a long time you may not realize what is going on. Rarely will a subordinate schemer do something so flagrant as to risk getting fired or even chastised. You are not likely to get anywhere with a direct confrontation: "See here, what is it you have against me? . . . Can we talk about it? . . ." The schemer's most likely response will be to pretend he or she doesn't know what you are talking about.

Instead of an unproductive confrontation, your best defenses are these:

OBSERVERS   Establish a network of friendly observers so that you always know what is going on behind your back.

This may sound a good deal more sneaky and cynical than I intend. I don't mean you need to have spies listening at keyholes or going through people's desks. All I really mean, essentially, is that you should not allow yourself to get isolated. An isolated boss is one who can readily be schemed against. Instead of letting that happen to you, make it a point to have frequent, friendly contact with subordinates, peers, and others in and around the company.

The woman lawyer accused of drunkenness saved herself this way. She had noticed for a long time that top executives seemed to be wary and standoffish in her presence, but she had no idea a rumor about drinking was in circulation. However, it happened that she was in friendly contact with an older secretary who had recently returned to work after many years of raising a family. The older woman seemed lonely, so the lawyer occasionally went to lunch with her. They talked companionably about their families, their off-the-job interests—and, among other things, their health problems.

One day the older woman asked, "Tell me about that ear problem of yours. Does it affect your balance?"

"Once in a while, yes. I'll feel dizzy for a couple of moments."

The older woman looked embarrassed, hesitated, then said, "There's something you ought to know. The other day I heard Mr. Pollock ask if you'd been drinking."

Now a lot of things became clear. The woman lawyer immediately went to her superiors and candidly explained the facts of her ear ailment. The drinking rumor died quickly. In time, through other friendly observers, she was able to track down the source of the rumor. She had the young man transferred.

The more friendly contacts you have, the less likely it is that things can happen without your being aware of them. Take the time to talk with people. Don't eat lunch alone if you can help it. Chat with the security guard at the front entrance, the part-time file clerk who is working her way through school. One of the worst mistakes anybody in business can make is to become a loner.

PROJECT AND PRAISE   If you identify a subordinate as out gunning for you, one of the best defenses is to get him or her absorbed and enmeshed in a special project. Make the person so busy and enthusiastic that there is no more time for scheming.

It may seem peculiar to reward somebody who is plotting your downfall, but I can tell you from experience that this is almost certain to work better than a direct confrontation or threats of punishment. Indeed, I'll go further. We saw in another chapter that public praise is a highly effective tool of leadership; now it comes in handy as a weapon of defense. Having given your plotting subordinate an absorbing project and having seen him well started and thoroughly hooked on it, you utter words of praise at meetings: "That advertising evaluation is turning out beautifully, Pete. Very interesting results, not what anybody expected. Let's have a talk about the implications someday soon."

If you are lucky, you have now changed Pete from an enemy to an ally, at least temporarily. If he is smart, he realizes what I've said elsewhere in this book: that you score points with management by taking on special projects. That is how you get noticed. Pete has a chance for some excellent personal publicity, and he is not likely to spoil it by plotting your ruin anytime soon.

FARMING OUT   Another defense against a scheming subordinate is to get him or her moved out of your department. However, the seemingly obvious approach—firing—is seldom the best. To fire this subordinate, you need to prove that the alleged scheming has actually taken place and that it has been damaging enough to warrant such drastic action by you. Marshaling such proof is just about impossible, since the very nature of scheming is that it takes place under cover.

Therefore, you will have to seek other approaches. If you can get the troublesome subordinate promoted or transferred out of your department, that can solve the problem for you—but it may only create a new problem for the next person who becomes the schemer's boss. Promotions and transfers are not always easy to arrange, in any case.

Try a different approach first. See if you can arrange to have this person farmed out temporarily.

This may work if the schemer has a skill that can be put to use in some other area of the company. Stay alert for word of projects calling for extra people.

I know a woman bank executive who did this with a younger woman who had long been angling for her job. The younger woman had managed to spread some potentially damaging stories about inept leadership. After putting up with the problem for a time, the older woman saw what looked like a temporary solution. The bank wanted to send a small team of people to sort out complications resulting from a problem loan in South America. The job was expected to take six months. The boss volunteered her subordinate.

"I was careful not to put it to her like a banishment," the boss recalls. "Instead, I made it sound like a special plum. I said I was offering it to her because she'd been doing good work and because I thought she'd benefit from the trip; she could learn a lot. None of this was a lie. She actually wasn't bad at her job. But my main motive, of course, was to get her away from my group for a while. I needed a break."

What she didn't realize was that the seemingly temporary solution could be made permanent. While the troublesome subordinate was away, the older woman reorganized her group so as to compensate for the missing member. In the course of doing this, she stumbled upon a new way to structure the young woman's job—a way that brought her under closer and more effective supervision.

The scheming did not stop right away under this new arrangement, but it was enfeebled in its effect. The older woman could handle it more easily. In time, it did stop.

If you can arrange a temporary farming-out for your troublesome subordinate, you may be able to use the respite in a similar way. Try to reorganize the work so that you and/or your observer network can monitor the schemer more effectively and closely. One way to do this is to require more frequent reports on the group's activities.

If you are lucky, the farming-out could turn into a permanent absence; your subordinate could see new opportunities or be invited to join a new team permanently. If not, at least you will be prepared for the person's return.

Defenses Against a Boss

There are two common reasons why a boss might scheme unfairly against a subordinate.

First, the boss is seeking a scapegoat. The department's work hasn't been going well, perhaps, and the boss is getting the blame. He or she therefore starts to manipulate events or appearances so as to throw the blame on someone else, a subordinate. "The problems of this group aren't my fault," the boss will say or imply. "I had an excellent plan worked out to improve our performance. But the plan is being undermined. My orders are being deliberately ignored..."

The second common reason for such acts by a boss is personal animosity—simple bad chemistry. Such animosity often springs from obscure sources. A subordinate being schemed against or picked on by a boss will often be utterly bewildered. "Why me?" the subordinate wails. "What did I ever do to make him treat me this way?" The answer may well be: "Relax, you didn't do anything." For it is a fact of human life that people sometimes dislike each other and cannot say why.

In the course of a normal business career you will bump against many hundreds of people. Most of these encounters will be pleasant and productive, but it is almost inevitable that you are going to meet some men and women who can't stand the sight of you, and vice versa. There is little you can do about such bad chemistry but accept it as a fact of existence, like taxes and head colds. If it happens between you and a boss, then you must work hard to escape its effects.

Here is what to do:

MENTOR Increase your efforts to find a mentor, if you don't yet have one. You need one badly. If you do have one, increase your contact with this man or woman.

Say nothing negative about your boss ("He's always sneaking around . . . I think he deliberately hid that last report of mine and then claimed I'd never written it . . ."). Instead, simply say in uncomplaining tones that you'd like your mentor to be alert for possible new assignments for you. (See Chapter 8, on getting transferred.) You might say, for example, that you feel you've learned just about all you can in your present job and would welcome a new chance to grow.

If the situation with your boss is so desperate that you feel you *must* mention it, do so only in neutral terms. "The chemistry isn't right. We've both worked at it, but . . . I don't think it's anybody's fault, it's just one of those things . . ."

By avoiding any kind of blame-throwing, you make it easier for your mentor to offer help. Though he or she may like you a good deal, you cannot reasonably ask for backup in an assault on your boss. Your mentor, too, has a career to worry about and won't want to be drawn into a potentially bruising fight. So be careful never to let the situation take on the appearance of a fight; keep it quiet, reasonable, and nonbelligerent. This way your mentor can feel perfectly comfortable about saying, "Why, sure, I'll keep my eyes open and see what's around."

<u>DOCUMENTATION</u>   As far as possible, document everything you do and save the documents in a well-organized way, so that you can lay your hands on any piece of paper or floppy disk as soon as you need it.

The object of documentation is to prove, if proof is ever needed, that you have been doing your job well.

A woman whom I'll call Pat found documentation valuable a few years ago. Pat then worked in an administrative office of a television network. The department's performance was poor and its costs were unreasonably high. This inefficiency had been tolerated for years, but the boom times came to an end for the TV industry in the late 1970s and early 1980s. Top management wanted costs cut and productivity raised. Pressure had been put on department heads, and those who couldn't produce were being warned that they didn't have much time left to turn things around. Among those so pressured was Pat's boss, a young woman who had been promoted too fast in the boom years and now was floundering, out of her depth.

The boss needed a scapegoat, and Pat was it. Pat was the department's senior staff member. She had been there longer than anyone else, including the boss. She was the team's actual leader, if not its titular one. It was she who saw to it that the work got done.

Pat was aware of the group's poor performance and thought she saw how to improve it. However, she couldn't get her boss to okay any but trivial changes in the way things were done. The boss was too scared to risk any meaningful innovation. Moreover, she resisted doing anything for which Pat might get credit. And so the team's work continued to be substandard, and its costs stayed high.

The young boss's excuse was that Pat, her second-in-command, was working against her. "Pat is jealous because I was moved in over her head," the boss would tell the executives upstairs. "She was expecting to get the top job herself. Now she's trying to make me look bad. She hardly does any work. She's away from her desk half the day, downstairs in the coffee shop, probably. And she won't follow orders. I try to make improvements but she wants to do things the old way, it's easier . . ."

When Pat's observer network began bringing her hints that this was going on, she began to save documents.

Her first step was to get a desk calendar—something she had never felt she needed before. In it she carefully jotted notes on her comings and goings each day.

She also tried to get documents to establish the legitimate reasons for her time away from her desk. In one case, for instance, she had to spend several mornings at an ad agency, conferring on changes in a billing system. She made friends with the secretary of one of the ad executives. At Pat's request, the secretary typed up a brief letter of thanks to Pat and had her boss sign it. The letter said plainly when Pat had been at the agency and why.

Finally, Pat adopted a practice of communicating with her young boss more often by memo, rather than orally. In her memos she continued to suggest changes in the way the department did things. She saved copies, of course. Sometimes her boss would return a memo with a handwritten rejection: "Doubt this idea would work" or "Let's wait before deciding on this."

Pat saved everything.

Finally, one day things came to a head. She was called in by an older executive whom she had eyed as a possible mentor. He was grave and uncomfortable. He said, "Pat, I've got to tell you there's been some talk. Your boss tells us you're uncooperative. She also says you don't do much work. I must say I *did* have a hard time finding you at your desk last week . . ."

Pat produced her letter from the ad executive. She also showed her mentor a selection of her memos suggesting changes. She was able to document that she was not only performing her job conscientiously but was actively looking for ways to do it better.

Her aim was only to hold on to her job. As it turned out, however, her self-preservation campaign succeeded better than she expected. She was promoted to department manager.

PERFORMANCE   There is one other powerful defense against a scheming boss. It may seem obvious, but I mention it because people tend to lose sight of it. It is plain old-fashioned fine job performance.

In the first chapter of this book I pointed out that merely doing your job well isn't enough today to guarantee your security. You *must* get involved in what some disdainfully call "politics." But just as it is a mistake to put too much faith in old-fashioned job performance, so it is just as much of a mistake to emphasize it too little.

You aren't likely to get far on job performance alone. Nor can you succeed on "politics" or strategy alone. The effective approach is a balanced one.

So while trying to develop strategies for survival, don't let your work itself deteriorate in quality. Don't let the strategic maneuvering overwhelm the job.

Every successful business person is involved in politics to some degree. But the smartest ones are careful never to lose sight of the reasons why they are on the payroll. Strategic career planning is essential for security, but it isn't what the company pays you for. Always bear that in mind. Maintain a reasonable balance. The moment you cease earning your salary, you become vulnerable to career disaster.

═Defenses Against a Peer═

Again and again in your business career—unless it is a highly unusual one—you are going to find yourself in situations where you and a group of peers are competing for the same rewards. These sought-after rewards may be only vaguely conceived. You compete to catch the eye or win the favor of a boss, for instance. Or the rewards may be narrowly defined and specific. Perhaps you compete for a promotion that is scheduled to be carried out at some clearly anticipated time in the future. But whether you are going after vague rewards or specific ones, these competitions among groups of equals tend to generate a good deal of rivalry. This is the kind of rivalry you can expect to encounter most frequently in your career.

To protect yourself against a Machiavellian peer, you can use many of the defenses I've suggested for use against a contriving subordinate or boss. Maintaining a good network of friendly observers is essential, for instance. So is good job performance. Documenting your activities can be helpful in some situations. Increasing your contact with your mentor is useful in almost any perilous situation.

But there are also some lines of defense that are of particular value against peers who compete unfairly:

POLITICAL EXPRESSION   Bear in mind that somebody who wants to hurt you can find ways to do it even though your job performance is excellent. This means you must exercise care in areas of your life that seem to have little to do with your job. As long as this rival of yours is out there cooking up ways to defeat you, you will have to give up some of the freedom of speech and action that you once took for granted.

It's sad, but it's the way the world works. When you become a rival's target, you become less free than the Constitution says you are.

You give up the freedom voluntarily.

That is, you do if you want to keep your job.

One thing you give up is freedom of association. Later we will take a more extended look at the problems that can arise if you let your personal life get tangled up with your working life. For now, I just want to point out that a schemer will look for vulnerable places in your personal life if he or she cannot find any in your work. You must lean over backward to avoid any act—even the *appearance* of an act—of which people in the company may disapprove.

For example, perhaps you have strong feelings about nuclear energy: you don't want to see it used to generate electric power, and you think the U.S. should dismantle all its nuclear weapons. If this is your view, this nation guarantees you the right to speak out on it and act upon it. You can join nuclear protest movements, you can march in parades, you can write letters to the editor of your favorite newspaper.

But if you've got a schemer after you at the office, you should be very, very careful.

At some companies, such a political view would have little or no effect on your job. But suppose there is something you don't know: your company has an important customer that derives income in some way from the nuclear field. Then what happens?

It won't take your rival long to start the news making the rounds among executives: "So-and-so was in that big protest march last weekend . . ." You're now in a dangerous spot. Any company with a substantial stake in nuclear energy will tend to look askance at a nuclear protester.

You may argue that you were only protesting against nuclear weapons, or that you actually favor nuclear generating plants in the long run but don't consider the technology safe enough yet. No matter. You can argue until you are blue in the face; it isn't likely to help you. People tend not to listen to fine points in arguments about emotion-charged issues. All that needs to happen is that your schemer learns about you walking in one small peace march with one small placard, and you've suddenly put yourself in an unfavorable light.

Assess the company and its top management, as far as you know them. If you have certain views about abortion, or about the political situation in Ireland, or about anything that tends to get people excited, be circumspect. Avoid public expression of your views unless you are perfectly sure you won't be walking into a trap.

Strong views can be held privately and can be discussed in private among family members and friends not connected with your job. Be satisfied with that much for the time being. Save the public proclamations for a time when you have a more secure hold on your job.

IN-COMPANY GROUPS   Similarly, be very careful about becoming associated with any group of employees whom some in the company may consider radical, militant, too fond of complaining, or simply too noisy. A schemer can use any such association to hurt you.

You must use your judgment about this. Again, it depends on the nature of the company and the views and feelings of the top executives. In some companies, for example, membership in or sympathy for a union is no mark against you. In others, it's the kiss of death.

As a general rule (there are exceptions, of course), association with a union won't hurt you in a company where the union has been long established and comfortably settled, and where union-management relations are cordial and cooperative, marked by a mutual regard for each other's problems. But you can get badly hurt if you get caught in a situation where a newly arrived union or its recruiters are in a tooth-and-claw fight with management and where the mere mention of unions makes the board chairman turn purple with rage.

In a situation like that, stay clear of the fight. You may be considered a part of management and therefore not eligible to join the union, but you can get unofficially wedded to it in other ways— much more firmly wedded than is good for your career. You might talk a little too sympathetically to some union people, for instance. You might have a drink with them so you can listen to their problems. You might agree to sound out somebody on some particular union concern. *Don't*—not unless you have a top executive with you all the way. For you can be sure your schemer is going to use this for all it's worth: "So-and-so is a union spy . . . doesn't really understand the management point of view . . ."

Similarly, stay away from any other group that may be an annoyance to management. Don't go to that meeting of the people who want free bus service to the company parking lot. Don't sign that petition about day care. Don't wear that lapel button grumbling about the company's investments in South Africa. Don't even accept the button from the person who wants to give it to you. *Stay away.*

People who try to draw you into association with such groups will assure you there is nothing to worry about. "How can you get in any trouble campaigning for gay rights?" they will ask. "It's a free country, isn't it?" Sure it is. But remember that you have given up some of your freedom because there is a schemer lurking in the shadows, waiting for you to make a usable mistake. Give that schemer nothing to work with. Contrary to what various kinds of activists will tell you, there is *plenty* to worry about. Namely, your job and career.

Don't fret over this abandonment of freedom. It is only temporary. And the cost seems small when you consider what it buys: job security and career hopes for the future.

LOOSE TALK   You must also be careful about what you say to people in casual conversation—even to people you consider friends.

A friend today may not be a friend tomorrow. This is a sad statement to have to make, but it is a plain, factual statement of the way the world works. If there is someone out to get you, that person could well work on your friends and perhaps turn one or more against you. Or a friend can turn against you simply by becoming a career rival.

People in the business world often are bewildered and stunned when a friend betrays a trust or takes an unfair and selfish advantage. A friend's knife in the back hurts more than any other attack, partly because it is so unexpected. But the element of surprise need not leave you completely defenseless—not if you learn to expect the unexpected.

Always remember that human relationships are highly unstable, volatile, and subject to constant change. Today the people in your office seem to be settled into a solid, dependable network of relationships. You can sort them all out neatly: these three are friends, those three are friendly but not close, that one is maneuvering for advantage, and so on. That's how it looks today. But if you expect it to be that way forever, you could be making a mistake of career-killing proportions. The relationships are bound to change over time. Two people who hate the sight of each other today could become best friends tomorrow. Somebody you like and trust today could one day turn into an enemy.

So watch what you say—to everybody. Don't make negative comments: "This company stinks . . . George isn't smart enough to handle that job . . . Just between you and me, I think Marcia will lie to you anytime she thinks it's to her advantage . . ." Particularly when you know or suspect there is a schemer around, avoid the kind of talk that can be twisted, exaggerated, or used against you.

Naturally, we all get unhappy from time to time. Though people are always urging us to "have a nice day," there are days when it is impossible. Things irritate and anger us. When things aren't going well, there is a natural urge to complain to anybody who will lend a sympathetic ear. Don't give in to this urge—at least not around the office. Do your complaining among family members or friends unconnected with your work. At the office, keep your own counsel.

CLIQUES Also avoid being drawn into cliques or gripe groups. When you are dissatisfied about something, it is a great temptation to join a group of like-minded people who listen sympathetically to each other's gripes. Such a clique may consist of two people or half a dozen. Though a clique has no official standing in the company organization, it may have a good deal of unofficial, coercive power. A schemer can use that kind of power to advantage—or, conversely, can twist your clique membership into a weapon against you: "So-and-so is always hanging around with that group of chronic complainers . . ."

I've said earlier that it is a bad idea to bury yourself so deeply in your work that you become isolated. Having a large number of positive, friendly contacts is not only good strategy but also makes life on the job more pleasant. However, be sure the emphasis is on those two characteristics: positive and friendly. As far as you can avoid it, don't let your name get associated with the kind of clique that exists solely for scheming or tactical purposes or that is held together by the members' shared dislike of somebody or dissatisfaction with something.

Cliques try to increase their size and power, just as all other human organizations do. Thus, it is a common experience in any office to be approached as a possible new recruit. Somebody sits down for coffee with you in an out-of-the-way corner of the company cafeteria, or suggests lunch in a cozy little French restaurant, or walks to the bus stop with you after work. The question comes casually: "What do you think of Marcia?" It may be as bland as that, or it may have a stronger negative tone: "That was a pretty dumb move George made this morning, didn't you think?"

You are being sounded out. Beware.

There are only two smart responses to such a feeler. One is to say something positive: "Marcia? Oh, I like her. Has a good head on her shoulders, from what I've seen." The other is to reply without actually replying: "Well, I don't really know Marcia. She's always pleasant to me when we meet, but we aren't in contact all that much."

These replies may annoy your questioner, who was hoping, of course, to hear something else. But don't worry: you have not made an enemy. Enemies are made by *unkind* words and deeds. The worst that can happen now is that the questioner will stop making opportunities to lunch or walk with you.

In return, you have gained peace of mind. You have made yourself a difficult target for a schemer. You are elusive; there is nothing to aim at.

This kind of constant wariness and elusiveness requires a good deal of self-discipline. There are some who come into the business world believing such self-discipline is too much to ask, and they give in to the temptation to air their opinions and complaints. I can't argue; it is, indeed, satisfying to speak out on what's troubling us. But the fact is, if you value your job, you must learn to sit on these natural urges—particularly when you become someone's target. As J. Paul Getty used to put it: "We do business quietly. If you want to shout and stamp, go to a football game."

11

Your Job and Your Personal Life

Throughout this book I've reiterated its major theme: that merely doing your work well isn't enough to guarantee you job security or a bright future. This dictum is perfectly illustrated by the plethora of problems that can arise from your personal life. No matter how fine your work is, it can all be for nothing if you allow your outside-the-office activities to get in the way.

For they *can* get in the way—so much so that they can trip you and bring you down.

It is obvious that the calmer your personal life is, the less likely it will be to send shock waves into your office life. However, I have never met anybody who enjoyed a perfectly serene personal life, and I am quite sure I never will. The lives we live outside the office are bumpy. We're up one day, down the next. We are always wrestling with problems of one kind or another: problems arising from family relationships, sex, money, social concerns—the list goes on and on.

These problems do not vanish when you step into your office. In this chapter I will urge you to separate your office life and personal life as much as you can, but you know and I know that complete separation is an impossibility. When you go to work on Monday morning you are the same person you were over the weekend—the same person with the same problems and concerns. The trick is to organize your life in such a way that its two major halves—job and personal—can coexist harmoniously instead of interfering with each other.

Many people seem to find that a difficult trick to pull off. It can indeed be difficult in some situations. But it *can* be done no matter how hard it seems.

Let me tell you the story of a woman whose personal problems nearly cost her her job, but who finally got her life's two halves working harmoniously. She was one of the millions of women who in recent years have tried to balance the conflicting demands of raising a family and holding down a full-time job. It can be worked out neatly, but it took her a long time to figure out how.

Jean, as I will call her, was in her middle thirties. She was married and had a daughter, aged about ten at the time I met her. Jean had spent most of her working career at one bank. She had been hired there as a younger woman, had dropped out of the job world briefly when her daughter was a baby, and now was back, holding a middle-management post and hoping for something better.

The people at the bank had been delighted to see her back after that baby-care period, for they were impressed by her abilities and had big plans for her. To their dismay, however, her performance started to deteriorate. At first her boss noticed little things: she often came to work late, looking tired; her customary crisp grooming became a bit slipshod. Then the problems grew more serious. She became distracted and forgetful, sometimes neglecting to issue instructions to subordinates and then looking surprised when jobs didn't get done. She also became irritable.

Jean's performance was being adversely affected by her personal life. One problem was her husband. He held a job at another bank. His salary was lower than Jean's—a fact that disturbed him a good deal. He wanted her to quit work. The reason he gave was that he thought their daughter needed more parental attention. He pointed out that their day-care and baby-sitting costs were high and constantly rising.

Jean refused to quit her job; she had invested too much of her life in it to quit. But in an attempt to satisfy her husband and assuage her own feelings of guilt, she went out of her way to spend time with her daughter. She would sometimes spend long evenings at school functions even though she was tired after a hard day at the bank, and then she would go home and take care of laundry and other domestic chores. Her husband gave her little help in all this because he wanted to make the point that she should quit her job.

Another problem was his constant telephoning. He was highly insecure. He didn't like the thought of Jean's spending all day with other men. He phoned her often at the bank to check on her. At first she was charmed by this constant attention, but when she began to guess the reason for the calls, they became an annoyance. They interrupted her work and disturbed her thinking. She tried having her secretary block the calls, but this only increased her husband's jealous feelings and led to bitter arguments.

Her performance continued to slip. One day her boss called her into his office for a closed-door talk. "Listen, Jean," he said, "there are all kinds of places you can go in this bank. I'd like to set some wheels in motion. But there's nothing I can do until you get your life pulled together. I don't know what it is that's troubling you. I'll listen if you want me to, but it's something you've got to handle. Whatever it is, you've got to straighten it out."

Jean tried for a long time, without success. She tried talking with her husband. She tried various new day-care and schooling arrangements with her daughter. Nothing helped.

Finally, she and her husband separated.

Her problems were alleviated in a short time. The harassing phone calls ceased. With nobody to criticize her and make her feel unnecessarily guilty, she made new arrangements for her daughter—arrangements that allowed a reasonable balance between Jean's parental instincts and her need for rest.

But now she found she had fixed up one half of her life at the expense of the other. Her job was going more smoothly, but her family life had been diminished. Life as a single parent was calm but lacking in fullness. She wanted male companionship.

She met another man and fell in love with him. For a long time she was afraid to marry him, for her previous sad experience had taught her that marriage and a job don't mix well in a situation like hers. Finally, however, after many discussions, she became persuaded that the mixture can be made to work if you go about it carefully. She remarried.

Her life began to work again. She is now in line for the title of senior vice-president.

Below are some insights that can be derived from Jean's experience, plus some others that didn't apply directly to her situation but may apply to yours. All of them spring from two fundamental axioms: your personal life and job life should be brought into harmonious balance, and where they don't harmonize, they should be kept apart.

═ *Intrusions* ═══════════════════════

If a spouse, friend, or any other person from your personal life begins to intrude too far into your job world, find a way to show that you need more distance.

It is not usually very productive to tell a spouse, for example, that you would rather not be interrupted by frequent phone calls at work. As Jean found when she tried that with her first husband, it only leads to hurt feelings, and is unlikely to solve the problem in any case.

Such a request, more often than not, will land you in a volley of unanswerable questions: "You mean you'd rather talk to your friends at work than talk to me? Your job is more important to you than your family?"

Since those questions have no good answers, your best bet is to see to it that they are not asked.

Instead of telling this person that he or she is intruding too much, find ways to demonstrate it without actually saying it. The next time a phone call interrupts you, for instance, respond pleasantly—and then invent a crisis. "Uh-oh, something just came up! I've got to go. I'll tell you all about it tonight."

That night, or at some other good time, explain what the crisis was about. Then say something like: "I hope you'll forgive me if I'm brusque sometimes when you call. I really do enjoy talking to you. But this new marketing project has us all so busy . . ."

═ *Moods* ════════════════════════════════

Jean not only had her husband intruding too much into her job world, she also allowed her own moods to intrude. She became irritable. Her personal life caused this irritability, but she carried it into her working life.

This is a very common situation. We all get upset occasionally, and people generally understand this and allow for it. Your office colleagues and superiors will probably forgive you a display of bad temper or a downcast appearance once in a while—but they won't forgive you, and shouldn't be expected to, if the condition becomes chronic.

If you are always glum, condescending, or ill-tempered—or, perhaps worse, if you keep people on edge by being unpredictably up one day, down the next—you will quickly exhaust the patience of those who work with you. Although your moodiness may result from personal problems, your colleagues will naturally associate it with the office. They will wonder if they did something to offend you. Or they will wonder whether you are unhappy with your work.

If you suspect that you are letting personal problems intrude on your job this way, ask a friend to tell you confidentially whether your behavior is troubling others. If you have no close friend at the office, do your best to assess yourself. Remind yourself continually that the people you work with know nothing of your personal problems and should not be subjected to them. By being considerate of those people, you help yourself.

═*Communication Outside* ═══════════════

One of Jean's mistakes was that she failed to tell her first husband enough about her life at the office. She allowed it to be a mystery to him. This gave him the feeling of being barred from an important part of her life, made him more curious and suspicious than he would have been otherwise, increased his feelings of jealousy, and of course magnified all the problems related to her job.

Don't allow your working life to seem hidden and mysterious to those who populate your personal life. Some will want only a few details; they will quickly become bored if you try to tell them more Others will ask many questions and won't be satisfied until you give them a pretty complete story. Whatever they want, give it to them.

Jean's difficulty with this was a common one. When she came home after a long day at the office, she wanted to forget her job for a while. She didn't want to talk about it. When her husband asked questions she would merely mutter in reply: "Oh, I had a problem with a customer . . . too complicated to explain right now. What's on TV tonight?"

The more secretive you are about something, the more people will wonder about it. The more your family members or friends wonder, the more likely it is that you will get tangled as Jean did in problems of jealousy.

Suppose you are expected at a long-planned family dinner, but then you suddenly get called out of town to attend to a branch-office emergency. This painful kind of situation is familiar to anybody who has held a job for any length of time. There is no known way to make this conflict fun, but you can markedly ease the distress by telling people all they want to know about the way you earn your living. If you have been doing that all along, family members at the dinner may be annoyed, but most will acknowledge that what has happened isn't your fault. If you have seemed secretive, however, you could be in trouble. People will ask, perhaps out loud: "Do you suppose this is *really* a business trip? Couldn't somebody else have gone instead? Why did it have to be this week?"

Communication Inside

Similarly, don't let your personal life look darkly mysterious to people at the office.

This doesn't mean you need reveal a great wealth of details. Most of your job colleagues don't want that. Most would be bored by long anecdotes about your family or an analysis of your young-ster's school performance. Most would be embarrassed and put off by revelations about your sex life.

All that is necessary at the office is to sketch the broadest outline of your off-the-job life—just enough to assure everybody that you are a rounded, flesh-and-blood person. People feel comfortable when they can assign you to certain familiar categories: "Ann? Oh yes, she's married, has two kids, or maybe it's three. Her husband is an architect, I think. She's a great skier—you'll never find her at home on a winter weekend." Just that sketchy outline, just those few sparse facts are enough to give people the comfortable sense of knowing what kind of person Ann is outside the office.

Conversely, people become uncomfortable when you make a mystery of yourself. "Ann? Frankly, I don't know what she does or where she goes at five o'clock. She could turn into a werewolf, for all I know." By withholding the few called-for details of your personal life, you make it virtually certain that people will speculate about you—and once they start speculating, their imaginations are bound to conjure up stories, some of which may be less than flattering.

By making yourself mysterious, you make yourself seem odd.

People in the 1980s don't demand rigid conformity in office colleagues. Indeed, we in the business world today enjoy remarkably wide latitude in our styles of living. But there *are* boundary lines, and outside those lines you stop being just "a little different" and become "strange." It is perfectly all right to be a little different, an individual. People will admire you for it; you may even make a career plus out of it if you handle it well. But once you get labeled "strange" or "odd," you are vulnerable.

Strangeness is never given openly as a reason for firing somebody or denying a promotion. "Sorry, Charlie, you're too weird for this job." You will never hear that, but the fact is that strangeness often *is* a factor in career disasters. People in business, as anywhere, like to work next to colleagues with whom they feel comfortable. A man or woman labeled "odd" has a heavy handicap.

Bad Publicity

Make sure your after-hours activities don't generate unwanted publicity for your company or yourself.

Most companies today try their best to keep their noses out of employees' private lives. What you do on your own time is your own business—but only up to a point. If your activities become public in some sense, then they may become the company's business.

For example, let's say you choose to lead a varied and adventurous social life. That is your own affair as long as it remains private. But if you get involved with somebody else's spouse and the episode becomes public, your job and/or future promotions may be in jeopardy. Business managers are not so naïve as to believe all employees live like Puritans, but most executives would agree that it looks bad to customers and others when employees get caught in careless or irresponsible behavior. Every company wants to protect its image.

Or let's say you choose to get involved with a political movement or activist group of some kind. In the last chapter I warned of certain dangers in this, particularly when a schemer is looking for holes in your armor, and also when you espouse views that are unfriendly to your company's own business activities. But let's suppose you have neither of these hazards to deal with. You belong, let's say, to an activist environmental group. Your employer, an insurance company, conducts no business that has even a remote connection with that debate. You're safe, right?

Wrong.

Membership in that group isn't likely to do your career much harm as long as you handle it quietly. You don't need to make a secret of it, for people don't expect you to be apolitical or to subscribe to any approved party line. In the business world today, wide divergence of political views is amiably tolerated as long as it is managed with common sense and discretion.

But if your advocacy becomes shrill and public, and if the company's name gets dragged into it, then what started as your own free-time concern becomes the company's concern.

Suppose, for example, that you attend a rally at your local town hall, and a newspaper photographer takes a picture of you waving a placard. The caption in the next day's paper identifies you as "Janice Carpenter, a product advertising supervisor at XYZ Insurance."

You are now potentially in trouble. You have allowed your company's name to be associated with a controversy that the company would vastly prefer to stay out of. It's true that the association is distant and indirect. After all, you haven't claimed that the company is for or against what you advocate; you have only said that you work for the company. No matter: that tenuous link is association enough.

If you are lucky, the worst that will happen is that your boss will call you into his or her office and tell you to cool it. If you are unlucky, a major customer of the company will turn out to hold views strongly opposed to your own. Happening to have lunch with the president, he may make his views known in ways that could damage your career.

Common sense is the best guide in situations like this. If you join a Fourth of July parade and march in favor of patriotism and apple pie, or if you spend some of your Saturdays taking orphanage kids to the zoo, nobody is going to get mad at you if your activity gets publicized in association with the company name. If there is controversy surrounding what you do after hours, keep the company name out of it. When people ask who you are, you're Janice Carpenter, private citizen, period.

═ *Company Facilities* ═

Many employees seem to think they have an extra fringe benefit not mentioned in the personnel department's official literature. That benefit is use of company facilities for personal purposes.

I'm not talking about common pilferage of office supplies and other valuables. That is plain stealing—and, as should be obvious, wins you nothing but a very small, short-term gain at the risk of a large, long-term loss.

What I'm referring to is a kind of unauthorized taking that seems less serious than stealing because there is little or no direct loss to the company.

The phone is probably the most often abused company facility. Nearly all but the very smallest companies have telephone contracts that allow unlimited calling within certain areas or under certain restrictions. Employees think, "We can make all the calls we want.

It won't cost the company a dime!" I remember sitting in a reception area once while the receptionist at the desk spent forty-five minutes on the phone with a friend. Having finally ended that personal conversation, the receptionist immediately called somebody else and said it was time for lunch.

Office copying machines are also widely abused. I know one man who used company equipment—on company time—to make several hundred copies of a newsletter for his college alumni group. A woman similarly used an office machine to make a thousand copies of a political funding appeal. Mailing privileges are abused in the same way.

This kind of behavior reflects a less-than-professional attitude toward the job. It looks bad. It is the kind of thing that can be used against you. It indicates that you have only a loose fix on the dividing line between your job and personal worlds.

Again, be guided by common sense. I know of no company that would object if you were to make or receive a few brief personal phone calls of genuine importance in a week. Top executives have personal lives too; they are aware that they can't expect you to be shut off from all outside contacts like a prisoner in a concentration camp. But practice moderation. Forty-five-minute personal calls on company time are excessive and ridiculous. As a rule of thumb, I'd set five minutes as the limit. If you are the one placing the call, state the gist of your message as succinctly as you can and then say good-bye. If you are receiving the call, speak pleasantly but also briskly, to indicate you lack time for chitchat. Save the chitchat for later.

And don't allow your office phone to become a message center for free-time groups you may belong to—political-activist organizations, hobby clubs, civic groups, and so on. It is all too easy to get into this trap. Other people in a group may not be easy to reach at all times, but your office phone is covered solidly and efficiently every weekday in business hours. If you don't answer it, a secretary or your office-mate or somebody else will. Knowing this, the members of the Westville Historical Preservation Society will quickly take advantage of it if you let them. "We'll meet for a drink before the meeting," one member will tell a group of others. "If there's a change of plan I'll call Joe's office."

Nip it in the bud.

Also use common sense in your approach to other company facilities. Probably nobody is going to care very much if you use the office machine to make a copy of your youngster's latest school essay to send to his grandmother. But all except the very smallest personal copying jobs should be done outside the office. Similarly, don't get into the habit of using office machines to type personal letters.

If you have a secretary or share in the services of one, be very careful about assigning her to handle personal chores for you. Don't send her out shopping for your youngster's birthday present. Don't ask her to address and stuff envelopes for your college class reunion.

In more affluent times some companies tolerated such improper uses of secretarial personnel. Some bosses abused the tolerance quite flagrantly. But those days are just about gone. A few top executives in your company may still send secretaries out gift-shopping or put them to work paying personal bills, but you should *not* assume you have such privileges. Except at the highest management levels, most companies today have cut secretarial and clerical support staffs to an efficient minimum. A secretary's time is too valuable to give to you. If she gets thirty-five hours' pay a week, she is supposed to spend all thirty-five of those hours working productively for the company.

═ Personal Rights ═

A large number of federal and state laws pertaining to employees' personal rights have been added to the books in recent years. These laws grant you certain rights having to do with your religious beliefs and practices, health, pregnancy, and a variety of other personal matters. You can demand these rights; nobody is allowed to take them away from you.

But if you want my advice, you won't demand them.

Instead, you should ask for them in a pleasant tone, as if they were not rights but privileges. Furthermore, you should go out of your way to make it easy for your boss and the company to grant them.

Let's consider the issue of time off for childbearing—one of the most troublesome personal issues in the business world during the past several years. Under the Pregnancy Discrimination Act of 1978, which amends Title VII of the Civil Rights Act of 1964, you are guaranteed certain rights as an employed woman if you become pregnant. The law says, in essence, that your pregnancy is to be treated like any temporary disability. In granting you the needed time off for the birth and recovery, and in welcoming you back to your job afterward, the company is supposed to treat you exactly as it would treat a man, for example, going into a hospital for an eye operation.

That is the law. The company must obey it. But you make a serious mistake if you act as though you take this right for granted.

Avoid an attitude that says you don't greatly care whether others are going to be inconvenienced, that you care little about the job or the group. Sure, you are entirely within your rights. The law doesn't say you have to care. But bear in mind a few other things the law doesn't say. It doesn't say your boss must put your name on the next list for raises or promotions. Nor does it forbid your boss to abolish your job the next time the department's budget gets cut.

To protect your job, show that you care about it and about the department. When you know you will need a pregnancy leave, give your boss as much advance notice as you can. Offer to train your temporary replacement. If you are troubled by morning sickness in a pregnancy and must sometimes arrive at work late, show a willingness to make up the lost time at other hours. Don't wait to be prodded into this; do it on your own initiative, and do it with a smile.

The same advice applies to a man taking sick leave or time off for religious observance. It even applies to your vacation. Don't just vanish for weeks, leaving half-finished projects and jumbled files that nobody else can sort out. Go out of your way to make sure your absence won't inconvenience people or hold up the group's work. Do this even though it means extra work and time.

Never become the kind of employee who is obviously out to milk the company for everything it is legally required to give. That kind of employee is always among the first laid off and the last promoted. Instead, act as if you care.

You don't have to fly the company flag from your rooftop, but if you show loyalty through practical acts of concern and consideration, you aren't likely to go unrewarded in the long run.

═*Planning* ═══════════════════

Finally, I would urge you to plan your own preferred mixture of job and personal worlds as carefully as you can. Don't just let it happen. Decide how you want it to be and then work to make sure it all runs smoothly.

This advice applies particularly to young women starting careers in this complicated world of the 1980s. Ask yourself: what is my adult life *for?* What do I want to dedicate it to? The three most common choices today are a career, a family, or some combination of career *and* family. Women in increasing numbers are opting for the combination. Some are finding ways to make it work. Others get into assorted difficulties and end with feelings of failure in either the job or home sphere—or, as often as not, both.

Careless planning often turns out to be at the root of the difficulty. If you are a young woman with a promising job and are thinking of getting married, be sure your prospective husband understands what kind of future you envision. Discuss it with this man until it is clarified for both of you in detail. Do you want to live in a city? Do you look forward to more schooling?

Or suppose you are already married and your husband suggests it would be nice to have a baby. Before drifting into that adventure, be sure he understands how you envision it. Does he grasp clearly that you don't see the beginning of parenthood as the end of your career? Does he know you expect him to take over an honest half of the parenting burden? Is he prepared to do that willingly? Does he understand that you intend to devote full time to your job on business days—that the child must be cared for by others much of the time?

Sort all these questions out *before* you make the decision. If you find that you and your husband cannot talk about the questions without getting into arguments, then it is obvious that a lot more discussion and thinking are required. You may decide in the end that, in your particular case, a baby would be a disaster rather than a blessing.

It may be painful to make this discovery—but not nearly as painful as to make it after the baby is born.

Meanwhile, you should be just as foresighted in the office. If you and your husband do decide a baby is what you want, start paving the way. Don't allow your pregnancy to take your boss by surprise. Let him or her know your plans as soon as you know them: "My husband and I hope to have a baby someday, but I'm planning to go on working..."

While waiting for the happy process to begin, put just a little extra time and energy into your job. Knowing that you will eventually need a childbearing leave and may be troubled by morning sickness or fatigue, prepare for that future by showing a willingness to do extra work now.

With a little bit of advance planning like this, you will avoid the sour kind of reaction that I heard recently from a woman executive. She ran a fairly large billing department, and in that department was a young woman whose philosophy was to do as little work as possible. The young woman came in one day and hit her boss with the surprise announcement that she was pregnant.

"I know just how this pregnancy is going to be," the woman executive told me gloomily. "Three mornings a week she'll come in late, and the other two days she'll go home early. And at the end of it she'll ask for the maximum allowable leave. She's got the company where she wants us: she has a *legal* reason for goofing off."

I can see that young woman's future quite plainly. The company will give her the childbearing leave, of course, as is her legal right. But at some time in the not too distant future, her boss will find an equally legal reason to give her her walking papers.

12

Sex on the Job

In a large international bank recently, a woman stock-market analyst had an affair with a senior executive. Her immediate boss ordered her to break it off, alleging that the affair was adversely affecting her work. The boss believed, among other things, that some of her stock "buy" recommendations were designed mainly to make money for her lover, rather than for the bank's trust-account clients. The boss's suspicion was that the executive, her lover, would quietly buy a sizable amount of stock and would then ask her to recommend that stock to the bank. The bank would buy its usual large amount, the price would jump, and the executive would happily sell out, pocketing a quick gain.

The woman analyst denied this. Her boss would not back down. He issued an ultimatum: quit seeing that executive, or out you go.

Instead of obeying that order, she went to the executive for protection. He managed to pull some strings and get her transferred to another job at slightly higher pay in one of the bank's branch offices.

So she won the game, right?

Wrong. The new job is a dead end. As things look now, the bank will never let her get back to her chosen profession of market analyst—and to make matters worse, it seems unlikely that the bank will ever recommend her for similar work elsewhere, should she decide to move on. She has been sent into exile and frozen. To complete her catalogue of misfortunes, her lover ended their affair. The executive, worried about the developing scandal and its potential effect on his career, let her know quite bluntly that he did not want to see her any more. He doesn't even return her phone calls.

Another recent case involved a woman sales manager at IBM. She had an affair not with a colleague but with a former IBM salesman who had quit and now worked for a competing company.

Her superiors made plain their unhappiness over the affair. She claimed later that they threatened her with a demotion unless she abandoned the affair. She refused to do that, but she also saw that she no longer had a future with IBM. So she quit.

And then she sued IBM for invasion of privacy and sex discrimination. She asserted that her lover still regularly lunched and socialized with his former men friends at IBM. Why were't *they* being punished in the same way? She felt it was unfair to single her out just because her relationship with the man had a sexual element.

A sympathetic court agreed and awarded her $300,000.

So she won—but not quite.

In the first place, IBM has said it will appeal, so it may be a long time before she sees the money, if she ever sees it. Moreover, it took her considerable time to find another good job. Two jobs failed to work out, and now she is in a third. It may be a while before she gets her career solidly back on the tracks. And finally, she, like the bank stock analyst, has lost the lover for whose sake she went through all this.

The moral of these two stories should be clear.

Sex on the job is dangerous. Play with it and you play with a ticking bomb. Unless you are lucky, it will blow up in your face.

It is expecially dangerous if you are a woman. It is *doubly* so if you are the junior-ranking partner in an affair between two people of unequal job level, power, and status.

══ *Changing Times* ══

Nobody who has been in the job world during the past ten years—indeed, nobody who has read a newspaper occasionally—needs to be told that the business scene is changing fast.

Some of the changes are real. Others are mostly illusions. It is essential that you see clearly which is which.

One of the real changes has been the enormous influx of women into the job world. Another has been the slow but steady expansion of opportunities for women at ever higher levels of rank, pay, power, and status. This expansion is by no means complete; women don't yet enjoy equality with men in all industries. But it has certainly progressed to the point where men and women are coming into contact on the job more and more often, in work situations that bring them into ever greater intimacy. These changes are real.

Meanwhile, there has been a lot of talk about some other changes: the seemingly increased "openness" of life at the office, the "relaxed social mores," the "vanishing sexual taboos," and so on.

Don't you believe it. Talk is what it mostly is. In large measure, the relaxed mores at the office are an illusion.

It is certainly true that social-sexual mores are less strict in the general society around us than was the case a decade or two ago. But to translate that change into the average business office is wishful thinking. You tell yourself bravely: "These are the 1980s! Everybody agrees: our private lives are our own, right? So I can have as many affairs as I wish, and the people in the office won't even raise an eyebrow."

Like hell they won't.

It isn't just that business offices are stuffy, slow to adapt to social change. That is true to a degree, of course. Some bosses, some offices, and some entire companies are quite stiff-collared in their approach to life. But that isn't by any means the only factor affecting attitudes toward sex on the job, and it probably isn't even the most important factor. More important are certain pragmatic calculations. There are sound, practical reasons why most managements discourage sex in the office.

It will pay you to understand this well. Business managers are not some peculiar breed of men and women with blue noses. They have sex lives like anybody else. (According to one psychologist's poll, in fact, business executives tend to enjoy sex more than people in the entertainment industry, who make a lot more noise about it.) So you shouldn't buy the common notion that business managers discourage sex on the job because they are mean, joyless, and puritanical. The facts are quite otherwise. Your superiors are against on-the-job sex because, having been around long enough to see what it can do, they have reached two conclusions about it:

It usually ends badly for the company.

And it usually ends badly for one partner or both. In other words, the odds are it will end badly for *you*.

The "True Love" Phenomenon

Before we go on to analyze the problem of sex on the job and the ways to handle it, let me acknowledge that it isn't *always* a problem. I'm aware, too, that it isn't always easy and sometimes isn't even possible to avoid having an affair in the office, that there sometimes doesn't seem to be any reason to avoid it, and that it *can* end well.

Whether you do or don't get involved in an office affair will be a matter for your own adult judgment. All I hope to do in this chapter is help you build a solid basis of information on which to rest that judgment.

As you are probably aware if you've worked in an office for more than a short time, powerful sexual attractions can spring up on the job—can spring up very suddenly at times, taking people by surprise. This is entirely understandable. People who work together develop a special relationship. This is particularly true when a strong team spirit exists. The office becomes a warm and cozy place. Your own success depends partly on the performance of these other people; their success depends on yours. In periods when the team is working on difficult and challenging projects, this interdependence grows more stark; the general emotional voltage increases. Lifelong friendships get started in that kind of atmosphere.

And so do romances.

If you and somebody of the other sex work together on a project, you can easily grow closer together than either of you expected. As the work progresses, you share disappointments and you share triumphs. Whenever something either painful or pleasant happens on the job, you feel—*and it may be perfectly true*—that nobody else in the whole world understands this pain or this joy quite as well as your office colleague. This kind of feeling can get translated into sexual energy.

If and when that happens, it will be your responsibility to yourself to step back and take a cold, hard look at the situation and its implications for your future.

If that other person is roughly equal to you in terms of job status and rank, and *if* he or she is roughly in your own age bracket, and *if* both of you are unmarried, then maybe you can hope for a tranquil, happy, and trouble-free ride through the tunnel of love. Nothing is guaranteed, of course. All I say is *maybe*.

Some office romances end with roses, champagne, and wedding bells, followed by a lifetime of shared joys. It happens more often in paperback novels than in real life, but it does happen. It would be a shame to miss out on something like that.

You can hope for some such outcome and, if convinced you can get it, go for it. You should know, however, that the deck is stacked against you. Most office affairs end far less well. That statement includes not only affairs based on physical sexuality alone, but also those in which the two partners feel a profound caring and a sense of shared destiny—the feeling that comes in a million different shapes but is usually called "love." You might beat the odds, but you should be keenly aware of what they are. Deep or shallow, most office affairs end with somebody suffering.

═ Hazards ═

Why is an office affair different from any other affair conducted away from the job? When you understand the differences, you will understand why most business managements discourage sexual liaisons among staff members.

There are three major hazards. They are:

Sexual and romantic feelings impede work. Put yourself in the position of a boss having an affair with a subordinate. The subordinate turns in a poor job performance. What does the boss do? It is extremely hard to criticize a lover—so hard that most bosses in this situation would avoid it. Others might try gentle persuasion of one kind or another, but the chances of getting any real improvement would not be good. Most likely, the boss's attempt at persuasion would end in an emotional blowup.

One way or the other, the poor performance would continue. This would be detrimental to the task group's work and the company's performance. It could damage the boss's reputation. And it might also have serious effects on the subordinate's future.

A perfect no-win situation.

An affair between people of equal job rank can also get in the way of work. Two people working on a project together often need to monitor each other's performance in an informal way. If one slackens off, the other finds some easygoing way to apply the needle: "If you're sure you're quite finished with your coffee, Joe, I'd like to get out of here before midnight . . ." But even this gentle prodding may be difficult to bring off between lovers.

More serious criticism may be more than difficult; it may seem impossible. In a normal work situation, if one team member begins to do really slipshod work, another member may feel moved to speak fairly sharply: "Joe, this makes me look bad, as well as you. I really need more accurate figures . . ." Motives of self-preservation help task groups discipline themselves in this way. When sex and romance get tangled up in a group's emotional engine, the objectivity tends to drop.

An affair can upset other staff members. This is particularly true of a boss-subordinate affair. The subordinate's peers may well suspect favoritism, for one thing. They may also suspect that the subordinate partner in the affair reports office goings-on to the boss. As a result, the subordinate partner may become an office pariah, feared, disliked, and isolated. The group's work can suffer badly amid all this unpleasantness.

Jealousy can also play a prominent role. I recall a painful situation in a large retailing company. A fast-moving senior executive started an affair with a young woman executive. As time went by she discovered that some of his power rubbed off on her, and she began to abuse it. She could occasionally use a company car set aside for him, for instance. She would offer rides to her office colleagues. She didn't do this with any intention of making them envious, but that was the effect. Moreover, she tried to boost her own authority by constantly reminding people of her special pipeline into top management thinking: "Don says . . . Don told me most of the directors think . . ."

She aroused so much animosity that the company finally had to transfer her to a distant divisional office. The scandal provided ammunition for some of the senior executive's enemies, who had been waiting for something like this. He had recently overplayed his hand in certain power-grabbing moves, and now his enemies were able to use the love-affair scandal as one last illustration of irresponsible behavior. He was stripped of rank and power, and he finally quit.

A finished affair can haunt you long afterward. Office affairs usually are short-lived. The typical affair has an exciting and hope-filled beginning, a difficult middle, and a disastrous end. And this is probably the worst problem of all: long after it is over, an office affair can go on causing you difficulties. The difficulties in this post-affair stage can be more severe, more painful, and more intractable than anything you experienced while the affair was going on.

If you have a love affair outside the office and it breaks up, in most cases you stop seeing the other person. This allows the healing process to begin. At least it prevents the emotional residue of the affair from nagging you too harshly or too often.

When an office affair breaks up, in the usual case you must go on seeing the other person. Not only that, but you must go on *interacting* with your former lover if he or she is a close work colleague.

This can be inordinately painful. It is painful whether the other person is your peer, your subordinate, or your boss. Particularly if the person is your boss, you could be in serious trouble. Your boss may turn cold, distant, or simply be too embarrassed to talk to you at all. The regular, effective communication that is supposed to go on between boss and subordinate may break down completely. Your only salvation may be to seek a transfer.

Before letting yourself drift into any affair, face reality squarely. Sure, the romance and the sex may be fun now, but ask yourself: *what will life be like for me when it ends?*

═Precautions ═

To protect yourself against these hazards, I suggest the following defensive measures:

Be careful about the signals you send out. Many men and women unconsciously broadcast signals that other people misinterpret as sexual invitations or encouragement. If you find your boss or a peer trying to initiate a sex relationship with you, ask yourself whether you have been sending out signals that you don't mean to send.

Clothing and grooming are obvious sources of misinterpreted signals. Obviously you cannot hide the fact that you·belong to one of the two sexes. But it is possible to dress and groom yourself attractively without overemphasizing your sexual qualities. My advice to both men and women is: dress like an executive. Make yourself look clean, crisp, and businesslike.

There are less obvious signals. Touching is one of them. Some people are natural touchers: while talking, they will touch a listener's hand; walking, they.will grasp a companion's arm or shoulder. This kind of gesture is entirely nonsexual. However, there are other people who are not natural touchers. To them, an innocent touch may seem to be a sexual gesture.

You can also send out unintended signals by what you say. For example, it is not a good idea to complain to office colleagues about your marriage or your off-the-job social life: "My wife and I can't seem to agree on anything . . . I'm having a terrible time with my boyfriend . . ." Such revelations, though spoken in a casual way, can be translated by others into meanings you do not intend: "This person is asking for companionship."

Broadcast cooling signals instead. Casually mention your spouse from time to time, in positive terms. If you are unmarried, mention a fiancée or friend of the other sex, even if you have to invent one. Carefully give the impression that you are *not* lonesome, starved for companionship or fun.

Don't be coerced into a relationship. Sometimes an unscrupulous boss will demand sex in return for job favors—or, in extreme cases, in return for the job itself. The victim is most often, but not always, a woman. She is particularly vulnerable in hard economic times. Her husband is laid off, perhaps. She needs her paycheck desperately. And so, choosing what she thinks is the lesser of two evils, she acquiesces to the boss's demand. "I didn't want to—I *had* to," she will explain tearfully later.

I've seen this unhappy scenario played out too many times. If you ever run into a boss who wants to play this game, my advice is simple and unequivocal: no matter what the cost seems to be, refuse to play.

For in the long run, you are unlikely to gain anything. You may seem to make a short-term gain: you keep a job you were afraid you might lose, or you win a raise or promotion you thought you might not get. But count on this: in the end, in one way or another, *you are going to pay.*

You will almost certainly pay in terms of a tense relationship with your boss after the affair ends. Indeed, you may finally be fired—the very fate you thought you were buying your way out of. On top of that, you may also pay dearly in terms of damage to other cherished relationships. If you are married and your spouse finds out, how will you explain it? Simply telling the truth as you see it— "I had to"—is not likely to settle the matter.

If your boss starts making suggestions and demands, first try to deflect them gently. If the pressure continues and there is no other way out, your only sensible defense is a flat, nonnegotiable refusal. Don't be rude or angry, but do be absolutely firm.

You *might* lose your job or a coveted promotion—but as I've noted, you might lose them at the end of the affair anyway.

On the other hand, your refusal may simply end the episode harmlessly. Your boss, bluff called, may quietly back off and never mention the subject again.

That is the only way to win in a sexual-harassment situation. If you adopt any other strategy, the game will be rigged against you.

Don't count too much on the law to help you. The law is undeniably on your side. Sex discrimination and harassment are illegal under federal law and most states' laws. If you choose to strike back against these unfair practices by suing your boss or the company, or by filing a complaint with a government agency such as the Equal Employment Opportunity Commission, you are within your rights.

Many people react by doing just that. The files of EEOC are full of cases filed by unhappy employees, mostly women, who have seized on litigation as the way out of an unpleasant situation with a boss or co-worker.

But the case of the former IBM sales manager, whose story I told at the beginning of this chapter, illustrates that the quit-and-sue approach gains you less than you may expect. In fact, I think it would be fair to say that, except in a very few cases, the person who goes to court or seeks government-agency help ends up losing the game in the long run.

For one thing, you will probably have to give up your job if you initiate any such proceeding. If you don't quit on your own, your boss or the company may find ways to force you out. Companies do not like being sued or getting dragged into bureaucratic hearings. Moreover, the company can justifiably ask how much time and energy you will devote to your job when your attention is focused on your complaint process.

So you are out of a job. Finding another one of equal pay and status may prove extremely difficult. Not only will you have to battle the hard economic environment that faces everybody else, but you will have some added handicaps. Prospective new employers will ask the same question your old employer asked: how much time and energy will you have to spare for your work? Moreover, they will wonder about your ability to control your temper. It may be unfair, but it is bound to happen. "This seems to be a litigious kind of person," they will say. "A troublemaker—the kind who goes to court at the drop of a hat. Why should we buy that kind of trouble? Who needs it?"

The complaint process is likely to be a long-drawn-out affair. It can drag on for years. You will find yourself endlessly filing papers, attending hearings, wandering through bureaucratic mazes. And in the end nothing may happen. The case may be dismissed. Your former boss may join another company. The proceeding may become inactive and vanish into the depths of a government file. Even if you win some money at long last, the amount is not likely to repay you for what you've lost and what you've been through.

The quit-and-sue approach is a last resort. When you have tried everything, when your situation has become intolerable and you feel that you are backed into a corner, then quitting and suing may make sense. But do be aware of everything it entails. Don't think of it as a handy remedy for casual use.

If a bad situation develops at your place of work, don't react in anger, storm out, and call a lawyer right away. For the chances are you will be able to fix the problem much more quickly, pleasantly, and effectively by cooling off and staying right where you are.

13

The Value of Varied Experience

The career of Martin R. Shugrue is instructive. He is Pan American's senior vice-president in charge of marketing. He got to that high post in part because, as a younger man, he deliberately set out to gain as much varied experience as he could.

He began his career as a pilot. Furloughed during a period of reduced traffic, he applied for a management job in which his pilot's skills would be useful. Thus began a remarkably varied career. He wanted to learn all he could, even if this educational process sometimes meant moving downward in job status. At various times he worked in labor relations, engineering, human resources, marketing. Finally, during a crisis, Pan Am found it had a critical need for someone with wide-ranging knowledge of many company functions. Shugrue was elevated to top management.

If you specialize narrowly, seldom looking out beyond the confines of your chosen corner of the business world, you can hope for a reasonable degree of success and security in good times. But when economic troubles loom, when crises develop, when companies are being shaken up, then it is the men and women of varied experience who come to the fore.

I urge you to do what Martin Shugrue did. When an opportunity arises to take on a new job assignment, don't just ask, "Is it a step up? Will it lead to more pay? Will I get a bigger office?" Also ask whether it offers a chance to learn something new. Will it expose you to some part of the company in which you've never set foot before? Will it enable you to understand functions and operations that have always been a mystery to you? If so, think seriously about taking it even if it seems like a lateral move, even if the work looks tedious and boring.

Benefits

Let's look at the advantages you get when you build yourself a background of wide-ranging experience:

KNOWLEDGE OF DETAILS AND PEOPLE   Very often the top management of a company will work out a grand design for improving earnings, getting the company out of a tight spot, or achieving some other goal. As everybody in business understands, however, a grand design is just a sheaf of paper until *people* take it over and bring it to life. Very large numbers of people may be involved, from managers all the way down to clerical and production workers—each taking some part of the design's broad intent and translating it into the details of his or her particular job.

Almost any time such a grand design is to be put into effect, there is a need for leaders of a special kind: people who thoroughly understand the jobs being done, understand the people, and understand the details. The wider your experience has been, the more likely you are to be seen as such a leader.

To illustrate, a medium-sized food-processing company decided a few years ago that there might be room in the market for a new, specialty breakfast cereal targeted at a particular category of adults. After commissioning a lot of market studies, talking to bankers about financing, listening to experts, and holding many secret discussions, the top management group made the decision to go ahead and introduce a new brand.

The grand design was complete. The problem was to find somebody who could turn it into reality.

Many well-educated, high-paid, respected people were available for the new brand manager's job. The advertising director was considered extremely competent in her field, but she knew nothing about production, shipping, or other areas in which problems always arise with a new brand. The production supervisor was also impressively bright and competent, but he knew nothing of advertising.

The company finally gave the job to a relatively young man who held a middle-management position in the marketing department. This was a man who had deliberately made his career an educational experience. He had originally been hired into the advertising department. Then, at his own request, he had been sent out for a year as an on-the-road salesman, visiting supermarkets and learning about food-industry problems from the retailer's special viewpoint. His old advertising job was not available at the end of the year because of a headquarters staff cutback, but he noted that production workers were still being hired. To everybody's surprise, he asked for a production-line job and spent a period with a blue collar instead of a white one.

And so his career went. Here was a man who knew people all through the company. He understood their jobs and the problems they faced. If the grand design contained some unreasonable expectations, he would be likely to spot that difficulty before it became a crisis. Conversely, he also had sufficient detailed knowledge to make the design bolder in areas where it didn't expect enough. The company's management felt he was the ideal man for the job.

Varied experience is so highly valued in certain situations that many companies make a formal policy of it. Procter & Gamble is one such company. People being groomed for brand-manager jobs and certain other positions at P&G must spend a year as on-the-road salespeople. It isn't optional; you do it or you don't move up.

"That year on the road teaches you all kinds of things you wouldn't learn in a classroom," says one former P&G advertising executive. "For instance, you learn all the reasons why a supermarket manager will give Brand A a nice eye-level display but will tuck Brand B into a corner of the bottom shelf. You learn about that supermarket manager's problems. Years later you think about him when you're making decisions about pricing, packaging, and so on."

LEADERSHIP   A leader need not necessarily be loved but *must* be trusted. As a general rule, people trust somebody who has a thorough understanding of the work they do—somebody who has done that work or related work himself or herself. They tend to distrust anybody who is moved over them with theoretical or classroom knowledge alone. Indeed, *distrust* may be too mild a word. *Scorn* is more like it: "Oh, sure, Elizabeth has a degree from one of those big business schools. Big deal. But what does she really know about the job?"

The more wide-ranging your experience is, the more likely you are to inspire trust through your actual, hands-on familiarity with the work being done.

This trust will grow in part from your own confidence. Knowing the job, you will know when it is being done well and when it isn't. You will know when it is reasonable to expect better performance. If the work deteriorates, you'll be able to say, firmly and confidently: "Listen, if you people don't cut the mustard I'm going to have to set up some hard new rules..."

You cannot easily do that when you are not thoroughly familiar with the work. You can only think, "Well, it doesn't seem to be going as well as I hoped, but maybe they *are* doing all they can..."

FLEXIBILITY   A wide range of experience gives you, finally, the ability to jump in many different directions as unexpected opportunities and hazards come into view.

No matter how carefully you plan your career, you cannot know how its course may be affected by random events beyond your control. Your company may run into trouble; your boss may be transferred; an executive recruiter may phone you with a stunning proposition. There is no way you can foresee such events, any of which could profoundly change your life, thereby dropping your carefully drawn career plan into the wastebasket. Since you cannot foresee these workings of chance or fate, you cannot plan or prepare for any one of them specifically.

You can prepare for them generally, however, by equipping yourself with a wide variety of job skills.

With a richly varied background, you put yourself in partial control of your own luck. You immunize yourself against bad luck, and simultaneously you strengthen your ability to take advantage of good luck.

If your job is abolished in some unknowable future crisis, your varied skills give you a good chance of latching on to another job in a different part of the company. If unexpected technical changes or shifts in management philosophy make one of your skills obsolete, you have others to fall back on. You are in a position to neutralize bad luck, whatever form it may take.

Or suppose a piece of good luck drifts into view. A recruiter calls, let's say. He is looking for somebody with certain qualifications. His client company is prepared to offer that person a wide-open future and a high salary. The more varied your experience has been, the more likely it is that you will fit the recruiter's specifications. Or let's say your company wants to establish a new task group to confront some developing crisis. The broader your base of experience, the more likely it is that your mentor will be able to propose you as the group's leader. It is a matter of simple statistics: the more you know, the better equipped you are to grasp good luck.

Getting Experience

One excellent way to achieve this wide-ranging experience is to do what I've advised in other contexts in this book: make yourself known as somebody who stands ready to take on challenges. Make sure your boss knows this about you, and make sure your mentor knows it. "I want to learn," your attitude should say. "I don't want to get too comfortable. Send me where I can be useful. Give me the chance to fail."

But that isn't all you can do. There is one other very effective way to get new tasks and responsibilities: *simply seize them.*

In any organization—business, military, government, whatever it may be—there are always problems that lie about unsolved. Sheer inertia keeps people from doing anything about them in some cases. "It's just something we've learned to live with," people will say, shrugging. In other cases, people may be scared away; the problem looks too formidable to tackle. In still other cases, a problem will persist because nobody has ever identified it clearly.

As an example of this last phenomenon—lack of clear identification—consider the story of a small Connecticut company that had a long-standing problem of low employee morale. The company's executives all assumed it was essentially a paycheck problem. Since the company was fighting for its life and no money was available for raises, the consensus was that nothing could be done about the problem until better economic times returned. The problem, therefore, was simply allowed to lie around and fester.

One young woman took it upon herself to find out what was really going on. Talking to employees at many levels of rank, she was surprised to learn that the size of their paychecks was not really a major concern. Most were glad to have any paychecks at all; they knew the company was struggling and were quite ready to wait until a more propitious time to ask for raises.

What, then, was the difficulty? It turned out that the employees' major complaint—the root cause of their low morale—was what they saw as management's aloof disregard for their comfort. They grumbled about a long list of mostly trivial inconveniences and indignities: an employee lounge and snack area were grimy and unattractive; some offices and work areas were poorly lighted; the employee parking lot was carelessly plowed when it snowed, and so on. The cumulative effect of these small problems was one big problem: a general perception of the top management group as distant and uncaring.

The indicated remedies were simple and inexpensive: a little paint, some new light fixtures, a few guiding words to the man in charge of plowing. The young woman not only became a company heroine but, in the process, gained experience in a field that was new to her: employee relations. Not much later the company merged with a larger one. She was made assistant to the personnel director and eventually moved into the department's top job herself.

What she did is what you should do: seize tasks and responsibilities without waiting for somebody to assign them to you. Obviously you won't want to do this so often and arrogantly that you turn yourself into the office busybody. Just as obviously, you must be careful not to act in such a way that people fear you are trying to move in on their territory. It is a good idea to check with your boss before and during any such move.

Be careful and tactful—but don't be shy. When you see a problem that needs to be solved, jump on it and make it your own.

14

Dealing with Recruiters

This isn't a book about changing jobs. Nonetheless, I feel you should know something about the pitfalls of dealing with executive recruiters who may call you. If you handle these people badly, you can jeopardize your current job *and* your future.

Once you have risen beyond entry level in the world of business—and especially if you have begun to achieve some personal publicity in the ways described in Chapter 7—then you may begin to receive phone calls and letters from recruiters. You may be startled and a bit bewildered by this at first. "Who are these people?" you will ask. "Are they on the level? How did they get my name?" It may seem to you that you are still a relatively unknown person in a relatively obscure job. Are these friendly-sounding recruiters genuinely interested in engineering a job change for you, or are you merely a pawn in some game that you are bound to lose?

Either possibility could be true.

Like any other field, recruiting is populated mainly by honest professionals, but it also has its share of charlatans. For your protection you should know and understand the way recruitment works.

A search firm may work either on a retainer or on a contingency basis. A recruiter on retainer is hired to fill a certain job or group of jobs—and, much like an attorney, is paid a stipulated fee plus expenses, regardless of whether the search is successful. A recruiter working on a contingency basis receives his or her fee when the search is completed; the fee is commonly figured as a percentage of the recruited individual's compensation.

Either way, however, the fee is paid by the company. It is never paid by the new employee. This is the first thing you should know about recruiters. In today's business world, no bona fide recruiter will ever ask you to pay a fee.

You should also be wary of any recruiter who wants you to travel somewhere but doesn't offer to pay your expenses. This is a sign of a recruiter who is trying to mass-market candidates. He may have a number of contingency assignments with companies scattered around the country. He may know little or care little about any given company or job. Instead, he counts on sheer numbers to earn him a living. If he can get enough people like you to travel at their own expense for interviews with his clients, some will land jobs and he will collect fees.

Unless a search firm offers you full travel expenses, go nowhere. A reputable recruiter doesn't mass-market people in that way. Instead, a sign of careful recruitment is the amount of work that goes into each search. A reputable firm is unlikely to ask you to travel anywhere until you have been subjected to long, close scrutiny.

Recruiters use many sources of information to locate qualified candidates. If I were asked to identify an engineer specializing in robotics, for example, I might begin by determining if there is a professional society devoted to that particular engineering specialty. I would then obtain a copy of the society's membership list. I would also go through trade or professional magazines in the field, looking for news items or articles by or about the kind of engineer I'm seeking. I would check lists of speakers at engineers' conventions. And of course I would seek word-of-mouth recommendations. I'd phone people who might be in a position to know the kind of engineer I want, and I'd ask over and over again: "Do you know of somebody who . . . ?"

The preliminary sweep in such a search can yield hundreds of names. A careful and competent recruiter does not simply submit this long list to his client, however. A long winnowing process now begins. Each name on the list gets a letter or phone call asking for preliminary information. More calls follow to those who are interested and seem to have the right basic qualifications. The most promising of these may be invited to one or more personal meetings with the recruiter. Finally a select few—*very* few, perhaps only two or three candidates—are invited to visit the client company for interviews. Their travel expenses are fully reimbursed.

If you are contacted by a search firm that wants you to go through a round of interviews, the chances are you are in good hands. The long, slow process shows care and professionalism. If a recruiter seems to be rushing the process, however—wants you to visit his client for an interview before he has even seen you— then you should be wary. This kind of recruiter may be playing the odds at your expense. He figures that if he can deliver enough warm bodies to his client, sooner or later one will get hired, and he will collect his fee without doing much work.

With those general points in mind, here are the specific strategic moves I would advise when recruiters call you:

Take time to respond carefully. Some recruiters make the initial contact by letter, which gives you time to do the necessary checking and thinking. Others prefer the phone—which doesn't give you time if you get flustered.

As soon as the recruiter has identified himself or herself, say apologetically that you can't stay on the phone, you're late for a meeting. Get the recruiter's phone number and offer to call back as soon as possible—or, if you prefer, suggest that the recruiter call you at home on a designated evening.

Whatever you do, don't try to respond right away to this initial contact. *Insist* on moving slowly. You need plenty of time. You have a lot of thinking and checking to do.

Check the recruiter out. It would be useful if there were one master list of recruiters, separating the reputable ones from the fly-by-nights. Unfortunately, there isn't. Therefore, you will have to do a certain amount of checking and sleuthing to assure yourself that you have been contacted by somebody who really has the potential to do your career some good.

One excellent approach is to question the recruiter closely the second time the two of you talk. Ask many detailed questions about the job being offered: questions about the company, the nature of the work, the reason why the position is open, the compensation, perks, and opportunity for growth. If the recruiter seems to know little, that could be a sign that you are being mass-marketed. A reputable recruiter gets to know a company and a job thoroughly before going out to recruit candidates.

Also question the recruiter about his or her own firm. How long has it been in business? Who are its bigger clients? Does it work on a retainer or contingency basis? Don't feel you are being too inquisitive. After all, it's *your* career and security that are at stake.

Talk to other people, too. Find out what is known about this firm, if anything. Be wary about talking to people in your own company, however. As we are going to see, this can be hazardous. In preference to that, talk to people outside the company who are in work similar to yours. Perhaps you belong to a professional society, for example, or know somebody who does.

Another way to get a handle on a caller is to find out whether he or she actually has an office. Suppose the pleasant-sounding woman from XYZ Associates gives a San Francisco phone number. Your indicated move: call San Francisco phone information and ask for the number of XYZ Associates. If the operator tells you no such company is listed, or if there is such a company but its phone number is different from the one you've been given, then you can suspect the woman who called you may be using her home or a phone booth as an office.

That doesn't automatically mean she lacks good qualifications. Ward Howell founded the recruitment profession from a New York City phone booth after World War II. But the profession has matured a good deal since then. If somebody lacks a permanent office, you should at least be wary.

Also be wary if you receive a letter with no return address but a post office box. That, too, could indicate the lack of a permanent office. Check with phone information to find out.

Also check street addresses in the same way. Suppose you get a letter on elegant stationery from XYZ Associates, with a New York phone number and a Fifth Avenue address. Very impressive. However, the address may be nothing but a mail drop, and the phone number may be a disguised answering service. The phone information operator will tell you if there really is an XYZ Associates at that Fifth Avenue address, with that phone number.

Be pleasant and cooperative even if you don't want to change jobs. Once you have determined that the person who has written or phoned you is genuine, be friendly and cooperative. Do this even though you aren't interested in the job the recruiter is trying to fill—even though, at this particular time, you feel happily married to the company you're with and are not contemplating a change.

Don't be curt or rude. *Make a friend.*

You never know how your situation will change in the future. A time may come when you may desperately need a new job. If and when that scary time comes, it will be comforting to have an active, well-regarded recruiter as a friend.

The worst mistake you can make with a recruiter is to wait until you are in desperate need and *then* send him or her your résumé. Every active recruiter gets a steady stream of unsolicited résumés. In difficult economic times, they get buried by them. Some are accompanied by letters suggesting hurry: "It happens I'll be in New York next week . . ." But even without such a letter, the tone of fear comes through. So does the whiff of incipient failure. Every one of these unsolicited résumés says, "This is a person on the way out."

I know it's unfair. So does every other recruiter. Not all résumés are from people on the way out. Some of the résumé-writers may simply be testing the water. Others may be in career trouble through no fault of their own. All the same, an unsolicited résumé always has that look of trouble. And a recruiter's first questions are: "Why is this person in trouble? What guarantee do I have that the same trouble won't repeat itself next time around? Am I safe in recommending this person to my client?"

Given two people of equal qualifications, one of them solidly established in a job and the other in a panic, a recruiter will always lean toward the solidly established person.

So take advantage of your happy situation now. A recruiter contacts you and tells you about a job opening in another company; you aren't interested; you're perfectly content where you are. Fine. But don't just send the recruiter away. Take time to talk about your career, where you've been, where you hope to go. If the offered job does interest you, go ahead and visit the recruiter's client company for an interview if invited. You gain even though you end up staying where you are.

You gain two things. One of them is knowledge. This contact with a recruiter and perhaps a client company is bound to give you some new insights into your job and yourself. The experience will help you arrive at answers to some of the job world's more baffling questions. What am I really worth? Does my job have a higher or lower market value outside my own company? How does my personal growth compare with that of others of my age in my field: am I ahead or behind? What kind of future can I realistically expect?

The second great advantage of this experience is that you gain a contact or several contacts. The recruiter has come to know you at a favorable time in your life, a time when you have a secure job and felt calm and confident. A time could come in the unknowable future when this happy situation changes: your job gets abolished in a budget cut, perhaps, or you get squeezed out in a power play. At such a time, with your world crumbling, you will need all the friends you can get. And there will be your friend the recruiter, ready to listen to you. Instead of being just a name on an unsolicited résumé, you will be somebody known and admired.

Visiting the client company for an interview could also have happy results. The executives who interview you at this calm and prosperous time of your life may be favorably impressed. They may remember you for a longer time than you expect. Several years from now, perhaps, their company will undergo a reorganization or a reshuffling of management, and they will need a new financial vice-president. While they are sitting around at lunch, wondering whether to promote from within or conduct an outside search, somebody will say: "Hey, remember that cost accountant who came down here for an interview a few years back? You know, the one we all thought was so outstanding? . . ."

Tell your boss about all such contacts with a recruiter. Whenever a search firm approaches you about a job you don't intend to take, find a casual way to mention the fact as soon as a good opportunity presents itself.

There are two excellent reasons for doing this. One is that it makes you look good. Your boss thinks: "Oho, this person is in demand from outside, it appears! Maybe we've got a more valuable employee here than we thought." (But see Chapter 7, on the technique of bragging without bragging.)

The second excellent reason for letting your boss know about recruiter contacts is that it is hazardous to hide them, or to seem to be hiding them. It upsets the average boss to learn or suspect that a subordinate is quietly looking for another job. One of the most damning accusations that can be thrown at anybody in the business world is: "He's interviewing!"

With some quick-tempered or jealous bosses, secret interviewing is a firing offense. "*Now* I know why your work is so poor!" the boss will say. "Instead of paying attention to what you're supposed to be doing around here, you've been spending half your energy looking for something else. Well, far be it from me to stand in your way! From now on you can spend *all* your energy looking . . ."

Even if it doesn't go that far, it can seriously set back your career to be caught looking around. People then assume you have lost interest in the job you now hold. Concluding that you won't be with the company much longer, management people stop thinking about you as a person with a possible future. Your name quietly vanishes from lists of those being considered for future growth.

There are some cases, it's true, in which a different scenario occurs: a highly valuable employee is found to be looking around, and the company, frantic to hold on to this indispensable person, offers a monumental salary increase plus a stock option, and use of the company limousine. However, this kind of outcome is much more common in novels and movies than in real life. Very, very few employees are that valuable. To count on it or even hope for it would be foolhardy.

So be sure to let your boss know about recruiter contacts. I said in Chapter 4 that, in dealing with your boss, you should carefully avoid any appearance of doing things in secret; and this is a prime example of what I meant. It would be bad for you, and could be disastrous, if your boss were to hear about your recruiter contact from somebody else. Right away your boss would think: "Interviewing in secret!"

Don't let that happen. Wait until a relaxed, natural moment and say, "Oh, by the way, I had a call from a recruiter—wanted to talk to me about a job with a Chicago bank. I wasn't interested, but I was surprised to learn the bank has more employees overseas than in Chicago . . ."

But keep a recruiter contact secret if you want the job that has been offered. This is the one situation in which I would advise you to hide your moves from your boss.

I offer this advice reluctantly, for it is always risky to do things in secret. But in this case you have no choice. It is a gamble you must take.

The gamble begins when you tell the recruiter, "Yes, that sounds like a job I could go for." It doesn't end until the recruiter's client company says, "You're hired." In the period between those two events—a period that can last months—you are at high risk.

During this period you must do a certain amount of tiptoeing around: talking to the search firm, visiting the client company for interviews, and so on. You cannot avoid this tiptoeing, for you cannot land the offered new job without it. If you are caught at it, however, you could lose your current job or set back your career with your present company. That will be no tragedy if you do in fact get the offered new job. If you don't get it, then you might be in big trouble.

So think long and hard before electing to take this gamble. How badly do you want the offered job? Does it represent a significant boost in income or opportunity or both? Or are you just looking at grass that seems greener on the other side of the fence? Consider these questions with the utmost care. Talk over the dilemma with those outside your company whose judgment you trust. Don't make a move until you are sure the potential prize is worth the risk.

If you decide it is, the recruiter will do much to help you preserve the needed secrecy. Competent recruiters are fully aware of the problems involved. If you request that all phone calls about the offered job go to your home rather than your office, any reputable search firm will honor that request. The search firm will also be helpful in getting you to the client company for interviews without breaching secrecy.

I recall an airline executive who was approached by a search firm a few years ago. The firm was trying to fill a job in a competing airline. The executive liked the sound of the job, but he was terrified at the possibility that he might be caught talking to his company's competitor. He refused even to travel to the competitor's head-quarters city. Instead, the search firm finally arranged interviews in a hotel suite in a neutral city.

That is how far recruiters and clients will go to preserve secrecy. You may not need to be as nervous as the airline executive was, but you should certainly be cautious—especially if the company offering the new job is a competitor of your present company.

Give the recruiter names of others who may want to hear about offered jobs. This will give you added help in making a friend of the recruiter—and it can also win you friends elsewhere.

A recruiter will often make the initial contact with you by asking for a recommendation. Instead of asking whether *you* are interested in such-and-such a position, the recruiter asks, "Do you happen to know somebody who . . . ?" This very common approach is really nothing more than a delicate courtesy. It gives you leeway: you can recommend somebody else, or—if it turns out that the job does interest you—you can of course propose yourself.

In other cases a recruiter, after getting to know you, will mention offered jobs that aren't likely to interest you at all. "Say, listen," the recruiter will say, "before we hang up, there's a job I'm trying to fill . . . I don't think it's anything that would interest you. The pay is below your level, for one thing. But maybe you know someone. I'm looking for a person with an M.B.A. . . . "

In either of these situations, when the job being talked about doesn't interest you, do your best to think of somebody who might want to hear about it. Your cooperative attitude will make the re-cruiter happy, of course. And it could also make a valued friend of the person you recommend.

When a recruiter asks you for such a recommendation, your

response should be: "Sure, I'll do some thinking. I'll call you back in a day or so." Then cast about in your mind: whom do you know, or whom do you remember from some past job or association?

As soon as you think of a likely candidate, give that person a call: "A search firm asked me if I knew anybody with these qualifications . . . I thought of you, but I didn't want to give anybody your name without your permission. Are you interested?"

You've made a friend even if the man or woman isn't interested. And think what might happen if he or she does go for the job and gets it. You have been instrumental in giving a career a boost. This person is not going to forget you. Years from now, perhaps, risen into a position of power, your grateful friend could be in a position to repay you handsomely.

15

A Crash Program: Pulling Through an Emergency

I said in the first chapter that you would find no Band-Aid approaches in this book. The principles I've outlined are all intended to build job security on a long-term basis. They may take many months to apply effectively, but once solidly established as part of your career equipment, they will protect and support you for the rest of your working life. No quick fix can offer that kind of lasting value.

But emergencies do happen, and there may be a time when you need to act very fast. Perhaps you have heard through the grapevine or have been unequivocally told that your department's budget and staff size are to be halved in the near future. Perhaps the news about the entire company is bad; it's common knowledge that operations are soon to be curtailed and hundreds of employees are to be laid off. Or perhaps the bad news is more personal. Your boss has told you your performance is unsatisfactory. You have three months to show improvement. If you don't turn yourself around in that probationary period, out you go.

In a situation like any of these, you urgently need a crash program. Your hold on your job has suddenly become very, very insecure. Looking back, you can probably identify a number of mistakes that have contributed to your insecurity—mistakes you would not have made, perhaps, if you had read this book years ago. You can rectify all those mistakes in the future, but that may take time. Your immediate concern is to get through the emergency that is facing you *now*. What are the measures that will bring fast results?

═ Special Projects ═

In Chapter 1 I told the story of Dan, who learned that a search firm was seeking somebody to replace him. Perhaps you remember Dan's response to this emergency. He devised a plan for solving some of the company's financial problems.

The first thing you should do when an emergency arises is emulate Dan. You may not stand as high on the executive ladder as Dan did, but that doesn't matter. Even if you are in an entry-level job and have no leadership function at all, you can still respond to your own emergency as he did, working with the facts of your own job situation.

Ask yourself: what does this company or this department need that I can provide? What does my boss need?

If you have been working in this job for a year or so, it is likely some ideas of this kind have crossed your mind before now. You've noticed operations in which money is being wasted, perhaps. You've wondered why a certain function always seems to take more time than it should. You've been annoyed by inadequate information on customers or suppliers. In idle moments you may even have toyed with possible improvements. You've asked yourself: "Why don't we do it *this* way instead of *that* way?" But you have not followed up on these thoughts. You have simply allowed potentially good ideas to lie sleeping in your mind.

Now is the time to seize one of those ideas and do something about it. Don't merely hand it to your boss in its untried form, but do as Dan did: research it, test it, marshal the facts to demonstrate its feasibility. Seize the initiative. Put in whatever extra work is required. Never mind catching your usual bus home. Never mind your lunch hour. You are fighting for survival.

Remember that if you aren't willing to give up some free time now, in a few months you may have a lot more free time than you want.

The project you choose should of course be one that lies within the scope of your job responsibilities. In previous chapters I've warned against the hazards of encroaching into what other people regard as their territory, and of playing with ideas that are too grandiose for your current position: "Mr. Smith, I've worked out a way to double the company's earnings!"

The project can be something quite lowly and simple. The only requirement is that it be genuinely useful. One woman, threatened with an imminent layoff during a corporate crisis, undertook to solve a problem that many people had found irritating. She worked in a department that made heavy use of certain business reference books. Department staff members had to go to the central company library to consult these books. Since other departments also had need of the books, they were often in use. Waiting periods of hours or even days were common; work was delayed; time was wasted.

The woman I'm talking about had often wondered idly: "Why don't we have our own department library?" Now she began to ask the question less idly.

Cost was the main problem. But when she researched the situation, she discovered that her department's main needs could be satisfied by only a dozen books. She estimated that three fourths of her own and her colleagues' library time was spent consulting just those few books—or waiting for them. Hence the department didn't need a full-fledged library; all it needed was one short shelf of books.

She went further with her research. She ascertained the cost of the dozen books. By conducting an informal survey of department staff members and keeping a record of her own hours, she arrived at a rough but plausible estimate of the amount of staff time wasted in waiting at the central library. She was able to show that, in comparison with that cost, the price of the needed books was negligible.

Her boss found her argument compelling. The department's efficiency increased markedly when the new bookshelf was installed—which made her boss look good, and also made it easier for him to cut the staff when orders to that effect finally came down from above. The heroine of the story kept her job, of course.

═ *Accelerations* ═══════════════════

While working on that special project, you should also pay close attention to certain precepts that have been presented in this book for nonemergency purposes. The particular ones that should concern you now are those that can be accelerated.

This doesn't apply to all the precepts, by any means. If you haven't been seeking education as aggressively as you should, it is unlikely that any panicky action on this front now will do much to save you from a firing in two months. You ought to think about education seriously when this emergency is over, but right now it probably cannot do much to rescue you. Similarly, if you have failed to cultivate a good relationship with your boss until now, you probably won't accomplish much with this problem in three months—especially in a crisis atmosphere. Instant, dramatic turnarounds in human relationships do happen, but not often enough to count on.

There are, however, some principles that can be accelerated with useful results. During this emergency period, pay special attention to:

GROOMING (Chapter 2)   This is one front on which you can achieve instant improvement, if you feel you need it. People often change grooming habits slowly, because it feels more comfortable that way and is less startling to others. But you lack the time to approach the change in so leisurely a fashion. Do it *now*. Show up at your office tomorrow morning looking crisp, immaculate, and ready for business. Stand erect. Speak briskly and confidently. You are under a cloud, but you must not let yourself show it.

CONTACT WITH A MENTOR (Chapter 5) If you haven't found a mentor yet, your chances of finding one hurriedly in an emergency are not very good. But if you have at least the beginnings of a mentor-protégé relationship, now is the time to accelerate its development.

TEAM PERFORMANCE (Chapter 6) If you lead a task group, do what you can to gain a quick improvement in its performance. Intensify your efforts to reward jobs well done, by praise or other means. If you have been putting off a confrontation with a poor performer, this is the time to get it over with.

USING TIME WELL (Chapter 9) This is another change you can make instantly, though admittedly it won't be easy. Start immediately to return phone calls and answer mail on the same day received. If your boss asks you to do something—even if he or she asks in a seemingly offhand way—do it right away. Forbid yourself to go home until everything you were supposed to do that day has been done.

POSITIVE ATTITUDE (Chapter 10) During this emergency period, be doubly careful about joining gripe groups or letting disparaging remarks slip out. The fact that you are in danger may make you more than normally sensitive or irritable; perhaps you feel anger toward your boss or the entire management team. But this is the very time when you most need to protect your reputation as a positive, cooperative, interested staff member. Don't slouch around, complaining. Don't mope by yourself, either. Go to meetings. Increase your participation.

OFF-THE-JOB ACTIVITIES (Chapters 11 and 12) Perhaps you have been involved in political, social, or personal activities that you've considered just a bit risky. You've continued with them because you have not noticed any tangible effects on your job or your career standing, but you *have* been aware of an element of risk. This assessment of risk should be doubled in your emergency period. If you are involved in any activity that worries you in the slightest, there is only one sensible response. Quit.

OUTSIDE CONTACTS (Chapter 14) Very quietly and carefully increase your contacts with recruiters or others who may lead you to a job in another company—just in case you need one. If you have not yet established a friendly relationship with a recruiter or other outside sources, then, as Chapter 14 emphasizes, this is a bad time to start sending out unsolicited résumés. Lacking such a preestablished contact, however, you can at least accelerate your studies of the job market as it applies to you. Get in touch with friends and others who may be able to advise or assist you. Think about what you will do if the emergency ends badly. And as one last item of preparation, study Chapter 16.

16

If All Else Fails

I t happens sometimes to those who least deserve it. You had
better be prepared for it, just in case. No matter how valuable
you have made yourself as an employee, no matter how carefully
you have followed the precepts in this book, you can still end as a
sacrificial pawn in a giant chess game beyond your control. You
will then have to undergo the most dreaded interview in the world
of business. Your boss calls you into his or her office, shuts the
door, sits, fidgets, and finally comes out with it: "Listen, I want you
to know how unhappy I am about this. I've tried everything I could
think of to find some other way . . ."

You're fired.

Now what? Do you just let yourself get swept off the chessboard
and into the discard pile? Or is there something you can do to help
yourself?

You may be surprised at how much you can do. Your actions
in the minutes, days, and weeks after a firing can profoundly affect
your future.

Calm yourself. It may take an effort, but it is the absolutely essential first response to a firing. Sit quietly. It may seem that the end of the world has come, but it has not. Hundreds of thousands of men and women before you have endured firings and survived. You aren't washed up—not if you keep your wits about you.

Don't be hostile to your boss. You may feel a lot of anger. That is perfectly natural and understandable. You may even hate the sight of your boss, may hate the entire company, may feel an urge to strike out at people. Suppress that urge. Having a temper tantrum now may give you some passing satisfaction, but it cannot do you any tangible good in the long run.

For you should understand that your boss finds the episode highly unpleasant. When he or she gives you the standard speech about feeling regretful and wishing there were another way, those words are, in most cases, the genuine truth. In all my time in the business world, I have never met anybody who enjoyed firing a subordinate—even a surbordinate who richly deserved to be fired.

By being hostile, by throwing a tantrum, you make the firing easier on your boss. This is exactly what you do *not* want to do. A case story will illustrate why.

The story involved a middle-aged executive whose career had been stalled for a time. He was considered perfectly competent but not brilliant. During a corporate upheaval, a new manager—a woman—was moved in over his head. As an indirect result of the same upheaval, one of her first duties was to fire him.

She hated the idea. She tried to find another opening for the man but could not. Finally, unable to avoid it any longer, she called him into her office for the unhappy interview.

She was prepared to be sympathetic. More than that: she was ready to lean over backward to ease the financial and psychological shock. If the man had given her the slightest encouragement, she would have fought to get him the best possible severance package, the most liberal terms for continued use of his office—whatever he asked for.

But he spoiled it for himself by being hostile. He shouted at her: "I don't need any favors from you! I don't need you or this rotten company! I'm glad I'm leaving!" Perhaps this saved his pride for a short time, but it did nothing for his bank account. The temper tantrum made the firing easier on his boss than she had been anticipating. Stung by his rudeness, she said, "All right, go."

He was given the minimum two weeks of severance pay and one week to clean out his desk. He is still unemployed.

The moral should be clear. Instead of being hostile, think of your future.

Use your boss's discomfort. This is the time to ask for a generous severance package and other sympathetic treatment. Your boss may have fairly wide latitude in determining what you are to get. Or it may be that there are company rules that can be bent under some circumstances. At any rate, you should *ask* for what you want. Ask for a lot. Your boss may seize on your requests as a way out of an unpleasant situation.

In all likelihood, when you react to the crisis by talking calmly and pleasantly about severance benefits instead of flying into a rage, you will see a look of profound relief on your boss's face. You have offered an escape. The chances are your boss will take it: "Of *course* I'll go to bat for you! Listen, I want to make this just as easy on you as I can . . ."

Don't let your pride get in your way. When you have a mortgage to maintain and mouths to feed and your own future is at stake, pride should be the least of your worries.

This doesn't mean you have to grovel. What it does mean is that you should take everything your boss offers and ask for more. Don't be too proud to ask for whatever help you want. Don't scorn it as "charity." *Take it.*

For you have a lot to do. Getting your derailed career back on the tracks will be hard work no matter how you approach it. But the task can be greatly lightened by the various kinds of help you can get from your company.

Don't just ask for severance money. That money is important, of course. The greater the amount, the longer you will be able to survive without dipping into savings, selling securities, or borrowing. Many people, in the panic of being fired, think of nothing else.

But there are several other benefits of enormous value that you should ask for:

☐ Continued use of your office or some other empty office, plus the use of the office phone. This isn't just a matter of convenience; it is a matter of psychological necessity. You will feel much better if you have an office to go to; it will make your hunt for a new job far easier. Moreover, it will enable you to hide the fact that you are jobless. As I've remarked earlier, recruiters and prospective new employers are always more strongly attracted to employed people than to those tainted with a suggestion of failure, no matter how unfair that may be.

☐ A mutually agreed-upon cover story. Prospective new employers may call your boss to ask questions about you. Prepare for this from the very beginning. Work out a story with your boss: you aren't fired but are leaving the company for some plausible reason.

☐ Consulting assignments, or some other kind of work that you can do for the company on an independent or free-lance basis. Less-than-boom times tend to increase the availability of such work, for as companies cut back on full-time staffs, many projects get postponed. You may know of such projects lying dormant around your company—and, if so, you will help your cause if you make specific suggestions about some work you can do. One young woman, fired from a Chicago ad agency, picked up so many free-lance assignments in this way that she soon found her income higher than her former salary.

☐ Direct help from your boss in finding you another job. Your company may have a formal "outplacement" operation to provide some such help, but you should enlist your boss's personal efforts in any case. Perhaps, for example, he or she can phone a few friends at other companies and get you in the door.

Those other companies might well be customers or suppliers of the company you are leaving. This isn't by any means an unusual situation. In one case I'm familiar with, a public accounting firm fired a young man whose flamboyant manner and life style clashed with the firm's sober image. His boss found him another job with a small client company—a group of entertainment people whose personalities harmonized perfectly with the young man's. As con-

troller of this little client company, the young man was now in a
position to turn around and do favors for his former boss.

Do your best to project confidence. This is one of the most
difficult aspects of getting fired. It is obvious that you must have
an aura of brisk competence and confidence in order to attract any
new employer. Yet it is this very aura that often gets destroyed in
people who lose their jobs. I find I can sometimes tell just by looking
at a man or woman—sometimes just by hearing a voice on the
phone—that this person is unemployed. Some indefinable depressed
quality seems to creep into the personality. You see it in the walk
and posture, hear it in the tone and use of words.

I won't try to tell you it is easy to maintain your confident
appearance. After all, you *have* received a severe jolt. What you are
going through is not a picnic. But I do tell you it is not as hard to
keep up that good aura as most people think. It can be done. I have
seen many do it successfully.

I've already emphasized the importance of having an office to
go to. This is part of a broader psychological strategy: for your own
morale and for its effect on others, *try as far as possible to behave
as though nothing has changed.*

Get up at your usual hour each morning and go to that office.
Don't allow yourself to mope around home. Dress and groom yourself as crisply as you ever did while employed. Carry your briefcase
even if nothing is in it. Have lunch with friends.

These suggestions are all endorsed by people who have lived
through the experience of losing a job. Among these people are
members of the Forty-Plus Clubs, a loose association of clubs set
up specifically to help men and women over forty who are looking
for executive-level positions. If you are under forty, your problems
may be slightly easier than theirs—but their advice is worth listening
to. It applies to anybody who needs a job.

One of the key Forty-Plus Club axioms is that moping around
home is a recipe for going nowhere. If you want to spend an occasional day at home composing a résumé or addressing envelopes,
that is fine—but don't make a habit of it. You will slip into what
one Forty-Plus man calls "the at-home mentality. You're in sloppy

clothes, you look like a hobo—and pretty soon that begins to show in your voice and attitude. You won't be aware of it, but other people will."

This is why Forty-Plus Clubs in many big cities have offices and telephones for use by members who can no longer use their former company facilities. There are strict codes of dress for anyone on club premises. These codes exist for one purpose only: to help members keep up their morale and project that essential aura of confidence.

If your jobless period outlasts your company-office privilege, do your best to find another office to go to, at least occasionally. Perhaps, for example, you belong to a club or professional society that maintains offices.

Beyond that, check your grooming every day with a critical eye. Check your posture frequently. Be sure you are standing erect, shoulders back, head high. And though it is difficult to hear your own voice the way it sounds to others, there are two voice qualities you can be aware of: volume and monotony. Don't let your voice die to a mumble or a whisper, and don't let it fall into a monotone.

People resort to all kinds of psychological tricks to maintain a confident posture, voice, and other subtle characteristics. One middle-aged man, during a jobless period, stood himself in front of a mirror several times a day and said, "I'm interesting! I'm valuable! I'm worth a good big salary! . . ." A woman went out and bought herself a bright red coat the day after she lost her job. She wore it to all her job interviews because, she said, "It made me feel peppy. I could never have gotten my mood up if I'd worn my dowdy old brown coat. That red coat was a big investment for somebody without a salary, but it paid off in the end."

She is happily employed now, as is the man who talked to himself in front of a mirror. You may not need to rely on such props, but these stories do illustrate the importance of mood when you are job-hunting.

Let things happen at their own pace. Don't be impatient. Don't pester prospective new employers or recruiters with frequent phone calls: "Has there been any decision yet? . . ."

Naturally you want things to happen for you quickly. It is not easy to hold on to your patience at a time like this—especially if the loss of a paycheck has put you in an acute financial bind that gets worse with every passing week. But there are three good reasons for avoiding impatience:

First, people are going to do things at their own speed whether you badger them or not. If a company needs three weeks to reach a decision, your thrice-weekly calls to the personnel director won't hurry the process one bit.

Second, impatience will undermine your own calm confidence—the aura that, as we have seen, is so important to you in this critical period of your life. If you give in to chronic impatience, you are likely to become visibly jittery and shaky. That cannot help your cause.

And third, your impatience will make a distinctly wrong impression on other people. Those too-frequent calls not only irritate people but, in time, take on the sound of desperation. It is a fact of life in the business world that desperation tends to turn employers away. The paradox is cruel but inescapable: the most coveted jobs, as a rule, go to those who don't really seem to need them.

So do your best to relax. While waiting for one decision to come through, explore other possibilities. Try to keep several possibilities alive at any given time. Keep yourself busy with family and friends. If you want to spend some time alone, don't get stuck in front of a TV set but go for a walk around your favorite city or a ramble in the countryside.

In time you'll get another job. And look at it this way: your career may have been set back or delayed a little, but now you have the grand opportunity to make a fresh start.

This time, let this book be your guide from the very beginning.

Index